An Edible Christmas

AN EDIBLE CHRISTMAS

A Treasury of Recipes for the Holiday Season

Irena Chalmers

Photographs by Amos Chan
Art direction by Richard Oriolo

William Morrow and Company, Inc.
New York

It is the policy of William Morrow and Company, Inc., and its imprints and affiliates,
recognizing the importance of preserving what has been written, to print the books
we publish on acid-free paper, and we exert our best efforts to that end.

Library of Congress Cataloging-in-Publication Data

Chalmers, Irena.
    An edible Christmas : a treasury of recipes for the holiday season / Irena
Chalmers.
        p.   cm.
    Includes index.
    ISBN 0-688-11084-3
    1. Christmas cookery.   I. Title.
TX739.2.C45C428   1992
641.5′68—dc20   92-17884
                                                                 CIP

Printed in the United States of America

First Edition

    2 3 4 5 6 7 8 9 10

BOOK DESIGN CONCEPT BY STEPHANIE TEVONIAN DESIGN

Contents

PART II: THE GIFT OF HOSPITALITY

Introduction

Christmas!

And everyone has arrived safely.

The frantic shopping and wrapping has all been done, except for that one last package that is still being wrapped at the very last minute amid shouts of "Don't come in—you mustn't see!"

It is Christmas morning and the coffee is perking merrily. The refrigerator is filled to bursting with such abundance that even the hungriest are at a loss to know what to choose first. There are brown eggs to be scrambled, oysters to be shucked, and white winter vegetables to be pureed into a mountain flowing with rivulets of golden butter. There are silken smoked salmon and sweet homemade blueberry preserves. There are jugs of fresh apple cider and jostling bottles of champagne, chilling. There are tomato juice and orange juice and grapefruits for squeezing.

Here are Virginia ham and thick bacon and a garden of mushrooms, flat and black, and brown, and tiny white trumpets, too. Sitting plumply on the top shelf, the grandest of turkeys awaits its stuffing with a bowl of cranberries at its side. The chestnut soup, rich and dark and ready for heating, is waiting way at the back of the middle shelf beside the traditional plum pudding. We have mincemeat pies and Stilton cheese and more and more tastes and treasures to be discovered and devoured during the day.

The counters are laden with round crusty country loaves. There are long skinny ones, too, and braided ones and black bread and bagels with poppy seeds and sesame seeds and blackened wisps of onions. There are fat, flaky croissants touching their toes and golden brioches from the bakery. There are apple turnovers and muffins with blueberries and muffins with pears and walnuts and muffins with spices. And soaring popovers still rising in the oven. And hot chocolate for the children.

The kitchen is the heart of the home, and it is there that many wonderful holiday memories are formed. Food plays such an important role in creating the Christmas atmosphere. There are dishes that we enjoy *only* at Yuletide—plum pudding, mincemeat, candy canes, certain cookies, eggnog. I know that I can never deviate too far from my traditional Christmas menu or my family rebels, as that meal is a physical representation of our bond through the years. In your family, you may find yourself making Grandmother's special cookies or copying The Way Uncle Bill Used to Roast the Turkey, and the day becomes filled with warm memories of loved ones.

My fondest hope is that some of the recipes in this book will become your family heirlooms to be treasured from generation to generation. I have had such joy in sharing my favorite Christmas recipes with you, and I trust that my ideas will inspire you to make variations of your own, both this year and in the years to come.

—IRENA CHALMERS

An Edible Christmas

Part I

GIFTS FOR SHARING

Two years ago, a friend of mine made a lovely batch of blueberry jam. As soon as it had cooled she poured it into attractive jars, sealed, covered, and labeled them, and sent them off to all her friends. She saved one jar for herself. A week or two after she had distributed her gifts, she sampled her own jam. Horrors! It hadn't set properly.

Last year she received a gift from one of her friends. It was a jar of blueberry jam. Though the label on the jar had been changed, she immediately recognized the jam as her own because it hadn't set. The message here is that if you don't like the gift of food you have received, take care how you recycle it. (Frankly, I believe my friend could have solved her problem by calling her recipients and telling them that she had mislabeled their gifts. . . it was actually blueberry syrup!)

Everyone will be happy to receive a gift of food, whether it arrives in the mail or you present it in person. There are many suggestions here for food gifts that you can—indeed, must—make at the last minute. If you are clever, you can cook several batches at once, thus saving masses of time and dishwashing. I do advise you, though, not to try doing too much at a time, but to do all the shopping on one day and then all the advance preparation you can. Chop all the nuts, grate all the chocolate, measure all the ingredients, and put them in separate containers. Line them up as though you were forming an assembly line. (Henry Ford was so smart about this sort of thing.)

Plan ahead, too. Don't find yourself with enough candy for twenty families and then realize that you have nothing to put it in and no brown paper or tape if you are going to mail it.

If, in a rash moment, you offered to bring something to your host for a party, and are wishing desperately that you hadn't volunteered because you haven't had time to make any of the gifts suggested here and simply don't have a minute left—do not despair. Buy something you like from a take-out store and add just one element that will make it into your own terrific gift.

Buy a mound of chicken salad, arrange it on individual red cabbage leaves, and garnish it with freshly chopped parsley.

Buy some ready-made guacamole and add a little fresh lime juice or hot pepper sauce and some salt (store-bought guacamole never has enough flavor).

Or start the dough for some yeast bread. Divide it between two or three clay plant pots, and cover with plastic wrap. Let the host put them on the table, where they will become a living, breathing centerpiece, rising nicely in the warm, crowded room—and if you are there long enough and they have risen for the second time, you can even bake them in your host's oven, and the glorious smell of baking bread will fill the house.

Or you can buy a great variety of fresh breads and arrange them in a basket. If they are not eaten, they, too, will make a beautiful centerpiece.

And if you don't have time for any of these things, just run to the Chinese take-out store and buy a hundred fortune cookies.

Four-Pepper Relish

Five-Alarm Salsa

Sweet and Fiery Red Pepper Chutney

Coriander and Pumpkin Seed Pesto

Classic Basil Pesto

Golden Peach Butter

Blueberry-Lemon Jam

Ginger-Pear Chutney

Five-Fruit Marmalade

Roasted Garlic Mayonnaise

All-American Barbecue Sauce

Oriental Plum Sauce

Onion-Thyme Marmalade

A Crock of Simmering Potpourri Spices

Puttanesca Sauce for Pasta

Flavored Vinegars

Rosemary-Lime Vinegar

Hot Chile Pepper Vinegar

Lemon-Garlic Vinegar

Flavored Oils

Walnut-Herb Oil

Provençale Spiced Oil

Flavored Vodkas

Lemon Vodka

Tangerine Vodka

Mint Vodka

Tarragon Vodka

Hot Pepper Vodka

Apricot Liqueur

Microwave Lemon Curd

Apricots and Prunes in Brandy

Chapter One

Gifts in Jars

The tradition of Christmastime gift giving takes on new meaning when your gifts are handmade. And since food is an equally significant part of the Yuletide experience, nothing is more appropriate or welcome than edible homemade goodies.

Some of the most coveted foodstuff gifts can be purchased from the shelves of your local specialty food store. But why purchase those pricey preserves, fruit-flavored vinegars, herb-scented cooking oils, spicy condiments, or brandied fruits when you can easily make them yourself for a fraction of the cost? Plus, you'll be giving your friends a personal expression of your affection. Here I offer some of my favorite food gifts, all packed up into bottles or jars.

There are two secrets to preserving in jars: organization and patience. If you think ahead a bit, you can have your entire gift list finished months ahead of the Christmas rush! Plan your preserving "menu" well ahead—summer is not too early; in fact, it is the perfect time. Canning jars are much easier to buy at the supermarket or hardware store in the summer months. Also, your preserving will be quite economical if you take advantage of the summer's lower produce prices. (Why buy enormously expensive imported fruits in December to make your gifts when summer's harvest was better flavored and a bargain to boot?) Giving a friend your made-by-hand, summertime Blueberry-Lemon Jam during a winter cold spell is like giving that person reminders of a sunny July afternoon—in a jar.

The virtue of patience is more difficult to acquire than the talent of organization. I am often too anxious to pop open a gorgeous jar of Apricots and Prunes in Brandy before its time, when I know perfectly well that if it sits for another week, it will be only that much superior. To avoid this dilemma, get your hibernating jars and bottles out of sight. After filling, pack the jars right back into the boxes they came in and store them in a cool, dark closet, garage, or basement until you're ready to give them. This will also save your pantry shelves from overcrowding.

Note that not all these gifts are meant to keep for long periods of time, and that some of them are refrigerated or frozen. Don't worry if a chilled gift is going to be out of the refrigerator for only a few hours. However, if you think your friend is going to let the present sit under the tree for any length of time, mark "Keep Refrigerated" clearly on the outside of the box and verbally tell the recipient to store it properly, in the box, until opening. (It's easier to insist, with a smile, that they open the box immediately and bustle the jar yourself into the refrigerator then and there.)

Here are some tips on how to successfully preserve your Christmas edibles:

Always use brand-new lids and rings. If you are reusing the jars, make sure they are free of nicks and cracks. Do not reuse mayonnaise or peanut-butter jars, as they are not made to withstand the high heat of water processing.

Wash the jars, lids, and rings well in hot, soapy water. To sterilize the cleaned jars, rings, and lids, boil them in water to cover for 10 minutes. Leave them in the hot water until ready to use, then remove them with kitchen tongs. Or, wash in a dishwasher and use them as soon as the drying cycle has completed. Always put up your edible gifts in hot jars. Bottles for vinegars, oils, and beverages do not have to be hot, but must be well cleaned and dried. You may recycle wine bottles with firm, uncracked corks. Look for imported, lovely new bottles with rubber seals in kitchenware and gift stores, or for an extra-special friend, purchase antique bottles.

Liquid and powdered pectin are not interchangeable. These recipes were tested with liquid pectin.

To fill the jars efficiently, use a wide-mouthed canning funnel, leaving ¼ inch of headroom between the level of the food or its cooking liquid and the top of the jar. After filling a jar, wipe away any spilled canning liquid from the jar's lip with a clean, hot, moist kitchen towel before sealing.

Some of the canning recipes in this book use the "hot water bath" method of preserving. (The procedure is unnecessary in recipes with a high sugar content, such as jams and preserves.) A canning kettle with a removable basket is the best choice for preserving, but any large saucepan with a rack and a tight cover will work. Bring enough water to a boil to ensure that the jars, when added, will have at least 1 inch of water over their lids. Cover the kettle and boil for the length of time indicated in the recipe. You should have enough water to begin with, but keep a kettle of boiling water on the side in case you need to add more to keep the jars submerged by 1 inch.

Remove the jars with a canning-jar lifter (with curved grips to avoid slipping) or kitchen tongs. Place the jars on a flat surface covered with a kitchen towel, and cool at room temperature for at least 8 hours.

Check the cooled jars for sealing. Remove the screw band, and if the jar is sealed, the lid will not slide if you try to move it. If the seal is not tight, use the food promptly, within the usual refrigerated shelf life of the food. If, after storing, the lid bulges or the food looks bubbly, do not serve or even taste it. Destroy it immediately in such a way that no person (or animal) can find and eat it.

If your food gift needs to be refrigerated or frozen until serving, mark the label clearly "Keep Refrigerated" (or "Keep Frozen"), and include a "use-by" date as indicated in the recipe.

The beautiful colors showing through the jars or bottles are often pretty enough, and your food present will need little embellishment in the way of wrapping. But here's one easy way of dressing up jars: Cut out 6-inch squares of Christmas fabric and center a square on top of a lidded jar without the screw band. Now, screw on the band, and the fabric will gather into a ruffle to add a finishing touch to your gift.

Four-Pepper Relish

I like this colorful condiment so much that I make it constantly to have on hand in my refrigerator. This sensational recipe was developed by my friend Stephanie Lyness for our book The Working Family Cookbook.

2 large red bell peppers, seeded and finely chopped
2 large green bell peppers, seeded and finely chopped
2 large yellow bell peppers, seeded and finely chopped
2 small fresh hot chile peppers, seeded and finely chopped
2 medium red onions, finely chopped
1⅓ cups white-wine vinegar
1 cup sugar
½ cup chopped fresh coriander leaves
2 teaspoons salt

Put the peppers and onions in a heavy enamel or stainless-steel saucepan. Add sufficient water to cover and bring to a boil over high heat. Boil for 1 minute, then drain well in a colander.

Return the vegetables to the pan and add the remaining ingredients. Bring the mixture to a simmer over low heat and cook for 5 minutes. Let cool, pack into hot sterilized jars and attach the lids. Process in a boiling water bath for 5 minutes. Remove from the water and cool completely at room temperature.

✂ *Makes about 3 pints*

Left to right: Sweet and Fiery Red Pepper Chutney, Oriental Plum Sauce, Four-Pepper Relish, Five-Alarm Salsa, Classic Basil-Pesto, Coriander and Pumpkin Seed Pesto, Sweet and Fiery Red Pepper Chutney

Five-Alarm Salsa

Salsa is an ideal last-minute gift. It takes almost no time to make and is ready in less than an hour. One of my favorite gift baskets includes a jar or two of my homemade salsa nestled with bags of first-class tortilla chips, such as the blue-corn chips available at specialty grocers.

1 28-ounce can whole tomatoes in tomato puree, undrained
2 fresh hot green chile peppers, seeded and minced, or ½ cup chopped canned green chile peppers
½ cup finely chopped white or yellow onion
2 garlic cloves, minced
2 tablespoons lime juice

In a medium saucepan, bring all the ingredients to a simmer over medium-low heat, then cook for 5 minutes. Spoon the salsa into hot, sterilized jars and attach the lids. Process the jars in a boiling water bath for 5 minutes. Remove from the water and cool at room temperature.

Note: The canned chile peppers will make a milder salsa than if you use fresh chiles. After opening, you can extend the salsa (and mute the heat a little) by stirring in a cupful of minced bell peppers or thawed corn kernels. A tablespoon or so of chopped coriander leaves adds a nice fillip.

✂ *Makes about 2 pints*

Sweet and Fiery
Red Pepper Chutney

Give this spicy chutney on its own or with a jar of Roasted Garlic Mayonnaise (page 17). It is excellent with grilled chicken or pork chops, but can be served as a dip with crisp fried pappadums—lentil-flour wafers that are available at Indian groceries.

2 28-ounce cans whole tomatoes in tomato puree,
    undrained
2 large red onions, finely chopped
2 medium red bell peppers, seeded and finely
    chopped
2 fresh hot red or green chile peppers, seeded and
    minced
2 cups cider vinegar
1 cup packed light-brown sugar
2 teaspoons hot or sweet Hungarian paprika
2 teaspoons salt
1 teaspoon chili powder

Put all the ingredients in a large saucepan and bring to a simmer over medium heat, stirring often. Reduce the heat to medium-low and cook, stirring often, until as thick as jam, and reduce to about 9 cups, 45 to 60 minutes.

    Ladle the chutney into hot, sterilized jars. Wipe the rims clean and put the lids on top of the jars. Process in a boiling water bath for 15 minutes. Remove from the water and let cool at room temperature.

✂ *Makes 9 cups*

Coriander and
Pumpkin Seed Pesto

Here is a variation on the traditional basil-leaf pesto—and every bit as tasty. Toss with pasta and grated cheese, or serve a dollop with grilled fish.

4 cups loosely packed fresh coriander (cilantro)
    leaves, rinsed and dried
⅔ cup mild olive oil or vegetable oil
3 medium-size cloves garlic, crushed
¼ cup unsalted shelled pumpkin seeds
1 fresh hot chile pepper, seeded
Zest of 1 lime
¼ teaspoon salt

Put the coriander, oil, garlic, pumpkin seeds, chile pepper, lime zest, and salt into a blender or food processor and process to form a thick paste. Transfer to hot, sterilized jars, label "Keep Frozen," and mark with a "use-by" date of 6 months after the pesto was made. Cover tightly, cool to room temperature, then freeze.

✂ *Makes 1½ cups*

Classic Basil Pesto

How fortunate we are that basil has become widely available all year round, at least in big-city markets. In the summer when basil is less costly I make masses of pesto and freeze it— and though admittedly it loses some of its brilliant color, it still tastes sensational and is a nice present to give along with a huge chunk of Italian Parmesan cheese.

6 cups loosely packed fresh basil leaves, rinsed
    and dried
1 cup olive oil, preferably extra-virgin
4 medium-size cloves garlic, crushed
½ teaspoon pine nuts
½ teaspoon salt
¼ teaspoon freshly ground black pepper
½ cup grated Parmesan cheese

Put the basil, oil, garlic, pine nuts, and salt and pepper to taste into a blender or food processor and process to form a thick paste. Taste and adjust the seasonings. Stir in the grated cheese. Transfer to hot, sterilized jars, label "Keep Frozen," and mark with a "use-by" date of 6 months after the pesto was made. Cover tightly, cool to room temperature, then freeze.
✖ *Makes about 2 cups*

Four-Pepper Relish, Five-Alarm Salsa, Classic Basil Pesto, Coriander and Pumpkin Seed Pesto, Sweet and Fiery Red Pepper Chutney

Golden Peach Butter

A gently spiced fruit butter that couldn't be better when spread on freshly baked Popovers (page 66). When summer's bounty is just a little too generous, this is a good recipe for using up those dead-ripe peaches, nectarines, or plums.

4 pounds ripe peaches, pitted and quartered
    (about 3½ quarts)
2 cups water
2 cups sugar
¼ cup lemon juice
Grated zest of 2 lemons
2 teaspoons ground cinnamon
½ teaspoon ground cloves

In a large saucepan, bring the peaches and water to a boil over medium heat. Reduce the heat to low and simmer, stirring often, until the peaches are very tender.

In a food processor fitted with the metal blade or a blender, process the fruit mixture in batches until smooth. Return the puree to the saucepan and stir in the sugar, lemon juice, lemon zest, cinnamon, and cloves. Bring to a boil over medium heat, stirring constantly. Reduce the heat to low and simmer, stirring often, until thickened and reduced to about 6 cups, about 30 minutes.

Ladle the peach butter into hot, sterilized jars, leaving ¼ inch of headroom. Wipe the rims clean and put the lids on the jars. Process in a boiling water bath for 10 minutes. Remove the jars from the water and cool completely at room temperature.

✖ *Makes about 3 pints*

Left to right: Five-Fruit Marmalade, Golden Peach Butter, Blueberry-Lemon Jam (in two jars), Ginger-Pear Chutney, Five-Fruit Marmalade

Blueberry-Lemon Jam

If you can get some of the tiny wild blueberries from Maine, they make the best jam. However, cultivated (or even frozen) berries are just fine.

4½ cups blueberries, fresh or frozen
7 cups sugar
2 tablespoons lemon juice
Grated zest of 2 large lemons
3 3-ounce pouches liquid pectin

Pick over the fresh blueberries to remove any stalks and rinse under cold water. Drain well and place in a large heavy-bottomed saucepan. (Do not rinse or thaw the frozen berries.) Crush the berries slightly with a potato masher or pestle. Stir in the sugar, lemon juice, and zest.

Bring to a boil over medium-high heat, stirring often. When the mixture reaches a full boil, cook for 1 minute. Stir in the pectin. Return to a full boil, then cook for another minute.

Ladle into hot, sterilized jars leaving ¼ inch of headroom. Wipe the rims clean and put the lids on top of the jars. Process in a boiling water bath for about 5 minutes. Remove from the water and cool completely at room temperature.

✖ *Makes about 6 cups*

Ginger-Pear Chutney

Here is an inspired recipe to keep in the refrigerator until you need to give it as a gift to the person you had forgotten until he or she arrives with something for you.

4 cups packed light-brown sugar

1½ cups white-wine vinegar

2 teaspoons peeled, grated fresh ginger

1 teaspoon salt

1 teaspoon ground cardamom

1 teaspoon ground coriander

½ teaspoon ground cinnamon

½ teaspoon ground nutmeg

Grated zest and juice of 3 limes

1 pound Bosc pears, peeled, cored, and roughly
   chopped

1 medium green bell pepper, seeded and finely
   chopped

1 medium yellow bell pepper, seeded and finely
   chopped

2 medium red onions, finely chopped

2 cloves garlic, minced

1 cup dark raisins

Combine the sugar, vinegar, ginger, salt, cardamom, coriander, cinnamon, and nutmeg in a large saucepan. Bring to a boil over high heat and simmer, uncovered, for 10 minutes to allow the flavors to blend.

Add the zest and juice of the limes, the pears, peppers, onions, garlic, and raisins. Bring to a boil, stirring occasionally, then reduce the heat to low and continue cooking, uncovered, for 1 hour, or until the chutney has thickened.

Remove from the heat and pour into hot, sterilized jars. Attach the lids and allow to cool completely at room temperature. Label the jars "Keep Refrigerated." Stored in the refrigerator or another cool place, this chutney will keep for several months.

✖ *Makes about 3 pints*

Five-Fruit Marmalade

A little effort yields enough marmalade to last a small family for a year, or provide quite a few friends with a luscious present. It makes a charming gift to fill a basket with the fresh citrus fruits and nestle one or two jars of the marmalade in the center. Slip laurel or lemon leaves among the fruit.

1 large grapefruit
2 large oranges
1 large lemon
2 limes
2 Granny Smith apples
6 cups sugar

Wash all the fruit well and dry with paper towels. Halve the grapefruit, oranges, lemon, and limes vertically through the stems. Cut the fruits into ¼-inch-thick half-moons. Remove and reserve the seeds.

Peel, quarter, and core the apples, reserving the peels, cores, and seeds. Tie all the reserved seeds with the apple cores and peels in a rinsed piece of cheesecloth. Cut the apples into ¼-inch-thick slices.

In a large, heavy-bottomed saucepan, combine the fruits with 2 quarts of water. Bury the cheesecloth packet in the fruits. Bring to a boil over medium-high heat, stirring often. Reduce the heat to low and simmer for about 2 hours, stirring often, until the liquid is reduced to half its original quantity and the citrus rinds are well softened.

Lift up the cheesecloth packet, press it well against the side of the pan with a wooden spoon to extract all the juice, then discard the packet. Stir the sugar into the mixture and continue cooking over low heat, stirring occasionally, until the sugar is dissolved.

Increase the heat to high and boil rapidly for 8 to 10 minutes, then test for setting. Remove a little marmalade to a plate and chill in the refrigerator for 10 minutes. (Move the saucepan off the heat while waiting.) When the marmalade has cooled, run a finger through the pool on the plate; if the surface wrinkles, it is ready. If it is too liquid, return the saucepan to the heat, bring back to the boil, and test again after 2 minutes. Alternatively, use a candy thermometer and cook to 221°F.

Ladle the marmalade into hot, sterilized jars, leaving ¼ inch of headroom. Wipe the rims clean and put the lids on top of the jars. Process in a boiling water bath for 10 minutes. Remove from the water and cool completely at room temperature.

✗ *Makes 11 cups*

Roasted Garlic Mayonnaise

This is only partially a homemade gift, but one that packs a lot of good flavor. The element you are adding—the garlic—becomes quite sweet when it is roasted. If you have a handful of mixed fresh herbs available, add these too. To extend the gift, fill a colander or a wooden salad bowl with a lovely arrangement of fresh vegetables and set the jar of mayonnaise at its heart.

3 heads of garlic (choose plump heads with firm, unsprouted cloves)
⅓ cup olive oil
⅔ cup water
3 cups store-bought mayonnaise

Preheat the oven to 350°F.

Divide the garlic into cloves, removing most of the papery outer layers, but leaving a thin skin on each clove.

Put the oil in a roasting pan and add the garlic. Stir well to coat all the cloves with the oil. Add the water and roast in the preheated oven until the garlic is very tender, 30 to 45 minutes depending on the size of the cloves. Remove from the oven and allow to cool.

Press the garlic cloves to squeeze out the roasted pulp. Force them through a fine sieve, or puree them in a mini–food processor until smooth. Stir into the mayonnaise until well combined. Pack into jars. Label "Keep Refrigerated," and mark with a "use-by" date of 3 weeks after you make the garlic mayonnaise.

✖ *Makes 3 cups*

All-American Barbecue Sauce

This wonderfully tasty creation comes to us from Philip Stephen Schulz and the late Bert Greene. It first appeared in their book Cooking for Giving, *and was preceded by this note:*

"If one had to choose a most 'typical' American barbecue sauce, this would be it—right down to the obligatory ketchup, Worcestershire, and A.1. sauce. It's a good basic all-around sauce. P.S. A batch may be made up in a half-hour flat!"

We pack this sauce into large jars for the barbecue lovers on our list.

4 tablespoons (½ stick) unsalted butter
4 medium onions, finely chopped
3 cups tomato ketchup
12 tablespoons brown sugar
12 tablespoons Worcestershire sauce
½ cup prepared steak sauce (such as A.1.)
¼ tablespoon cider vinegar
1 cup water
¼ teaspoon hot pepper sauce

Heat the butter in a medium-sized saucepan over medium-low heat. Add the onions and cook for about 5 minutes, but do not allow them to brown. Stir in the remaining ingredients. Bring to a boil over high heat, then reduce the heat and simmer, stirring occasionally, for 20 minutes. Pour into hot, sterilized jars and attach the lids. Process in a boiling water bath for 10 minutes. Remove from the water, and allow to cool completely at room temperature.

✖ *Makes about 6 cups*

Left to right: Onion-Thyme Marmalade, Roasted Garlic Mayonnaise, Oriental Plum Sauce, All-American Barbecue Sauce, A Crock of Simmering Potpourri Spices

Oriental Plum Sauce

Plum sauce has a splendid piquancy and will be a welcome gift for anyone who likes spicy food. It keeps well in the refrigerator and is an excellent dipping sauce for chicken wings and fried dumplings from the Chinese take-out restaurant.

8 large black plums, pitted and coarsely chopped
    (about 1¾ pounds)
1 cup dried apricots, coarsely chopped
½ cup cold water
3 tablespoons minced crystallized ginger
2 garlic cloves, minced
½ teaspoon salt
1 cup cider vinegar
⅔ cup sugar

In a medium saucepan, combine the plums, apricots, water, ginger, garlic, and salt. Bring to a simmer over medium-low heat and cook, stirring often, uncovered, for about 15 minutes, until the fruit is very soft. Stir in the vinegar and sugar and continue cooking until very thick, about an additional 15 minutes.

In a food processor, process the sauce until smooth. Ladle into hot, sterilized jars, leaving ¼ inch of headroom. Wipe the rims clean and put the lids on the jars. Process in a boiling water bath for 10 minutes. Remove from the water and cool completely at room temperature.

✗ *Makes about 5 cups*

Onion-Thyme Marmalade

This invention of what is affectionately known as new American cuisine is served as a condiment for cold roast chicken, cold meats, or cheese; it can also accompany curried dishes as a chutney.

6 tablespoons (¾ stick) unsalted butter
6 large yellow onions, peeled, halved, and thinly
    sliced
3 large red onions, peeled, halved, and thinly
    sliced
3 tablespoons white-wine vinegar
3 tablespoons brown sugar
1 tablespoon soy sauce
¼ tablespoon fresh thyme leaves or 1 teaspoon
    dried thyme
¼ teaspoon freshly ground black pepper
Fresh thyme sprigs

Melt the butter in a medium-sized saucepan over low heat. Add the onions, vinegar, sugar, soy sauce, thyme leaves and pepper. Cook, stirring occasionally, for 45 to 60 minutes, or until the onions have caramelized.

Spoon into hot, sterilized jars. Tuck the thyme sprigs into the sides of the jars. Cover and allow to cool at room temperature. Label "Keep Refrigerated," and mark with a "use-by" date of 2 weeks after the marmalade was made. Keep refrigerated until ready to give. The marmalade is best reheated and served warm.

✗ *Makes 2 pints*

A Crock of Simmering Potpourri Spices

Put this heady mixture into an earthenware or painted crock for your friends. This isn't exactly an edible recipe, but ⅓ cup of these spices simmered in a saucepan of water will scent the house with deliciously spicy aromas associated with the holidays.

4 oranges
4 tangerines
4 lemons
24 3-inch cinnamon sticks, broken into 1-inch
   lengths
¼ cup whole cloves
¼ cup juniper berries
2 teaspoons ground nutmeg

Remove the zests from the fruits with a vegetable peeler and place on a baking sheet. Place the baking sheet in a turned-off gas oven and let the zests stand overnight, or until dried. (If you have an electric oven, warm the oven at 200° F. for 10 minutes, then turn off.) Combine all the ingredients in an airtight container.

✘ *Makes about 1½ cups*

Puttanesca Sauce for Pasta

You may want to assemble a basket of foods from Italy along with your homemade sauce. Add a box of spaghetti or macaroni, some imported Parmigiano cheese and a bottle of Italian red wine. Tie it all together with green, white, and red ribbons, and if you are able to find an Italian newspaper or magazine, slip that into the basket as well.

¼ cup olive oil

1 2-ounce can anchovy fillets, drained and finely chopped

6 garlic cloves, minced

3 small dried hot red peppers, crumbled

2 28-ounce cans whole tomatoes in tomato puree, undrained

6 tablespoons capers, rinsed and drained

12 ounces black Mediterranean olives, such as Calamata, pitted and coarsely chopped (about 2 cups)

In a medium saucepan, heat the oil over medium heat. Add the anchovies, garlic, and crumbled peppers, and cook, stirring often, just until the garlic is softened, about 2 minutes. Add the tomatoes with their puree and bring to a boil, stirring to break up the tomatoes. Reduce the heat to medium-low and cook until slightly thickened, about 15 minutes. Stir in the capers and olives.

Ladle the sauce into hot, sterilized jars, leaving ¼ inch of headroom. Wipe the rims clean and put the lids on top of the jars. Process in a boiling water bath for 5 minutes. Remove from the water and cool completely at room temperature. Label "Keep Refrigerated," and mark with a "use-by" date of 4 weeks after the day the sauce was made.

✖ *Makes about 8 cups*

Flavored Vinegars

Flavored vinegars look sensational in antique bottles—or maybe even just old ones that you may find at a country fair. You can experiment with all sorts of different herbs, berries, or types of vinegars and oils, using this recipe and the one that follows as a base. Just be sure to store the vinegar or oil, tightly closed, for at least 2 weeks before tasting it and making your final decision. Whether or not to strain your gift before presenting it is up to you and depends on how enticing the flavorings look; prolonged immersion suits some better than others.

Give this vinegar alone or with a bottle of the best olive oil you can find. If you want to mail it, pack it, cushioned with straw, into the kind of heavy mailing tube that artists use for sending out rolled-up posters.

Rosemary-Lime Vinegar

4 cups white-wine vinegar, plus more, if needed
3 cloves garlic
6 large sprigs fresh rosemary
1 lime, thinly sliced

Two hints before you start: Use a stainless-steel saucepan when heating the vinegar to avoid producing a metallic taste. Take care not to cut the surface of the garlic cloves because contact with the garlic juice will cause the vinegar to become cloudy.

Bring the vinegar slowly to a boil in a saucepan over moderate heat.

Peel the garlic cloves, but do not cut them. Place a clove in each of two 1-pint hot, sterilized bottles. Carefully strain the hot vinegar into the bottles and add 3 rosemary sprigs to each. Divide the slices of lime between the bottles and seal each bottle with its cork or cap. Heat more vinegar and add to the bottle, if needed, to fill completely.

Store in a cool dry place for at least 2 weeks before using. For best results, use within 6 months.

Variations: To make Hot Chile-Pepper Vinegar, substitute 2 (or more) jalapeño chiles for the rosemary and bring to a boil in the vinegar. Add them to the bottles along with the garlic cloves. Seal, label, and store as before. (If you leave the chiles in the vinegar, the recipient will know that you intend ''Hot'' to be taken seriously.)

To make Lemon-Garlic Vinegar, substitute one sliced lemon for the lime, and delete the rosemary.
✘ *Makes 2 1-pint bottles*

Flavored Oils

What an attractive gift this makes—along with a jar of flavored vinegar and a pot of fresh herbs. You could make a theme gift, too, by including two or more salad plates or bowls or a salad spinner.

....

Walnut-Herb Oil

3 cups olive oil, plus more, if needed
1 cup walnut oil
3 juniper berries
3 walnut halves
6 black peppercorns
1 bay leaf
2 cloves garlic, peeled
2 sprigs fresh tarragon
2 large sprigs fresh rosemary

Pour the oils into two 1-pint bottles and add the remaining ingredients. Add more olive oil to fill, if necessary. Seal with a tight-fitting lid or cork and invert the jar several times to combine the ingredients.

Store in a cool dry place for at least 2 weeks before using. For best results, use within 6 months.

Variation: To make Provençale Spiced Oil, use 4 cups of olive oil and add 6 tablespoons mixed dried peppercorns (pink, white, green, black), 2 sprigs fresh thyme, and 2 cloves garlic, peeled. Follow the recipe as above.

✕ *Makes 2 1-pint bottles*

Left to right: Walnut-Herb Oil, Lemon Garlic Vinegar, Provençale Spiced Oil, Rosemary-Lime Vinegar

Flavored Vodkas

Flavored vodkas are a specialty at our house. I keep three or four different kinds in the freezer and serve them in small silver liqueur cups. These wonderfully intense libations were devised by Philip Stephen Schulz for one of the first books my company published, Vodka 'n' Vittles, *and he has generously given me permission to pass them on to you. Each recipe uses a fifth, or a 750-ml bottle, of vodka, and you can usually perform the alchemy of flavoring the vodka in the original bottles. It is a nice idea, though, to present them in antique bottles (or modern decanters).*

....

Lemon Vodka

1 small lemon
1 fifth (750 ml) vodka

Using a vegetable peeler, remove the zest from the lemon. Drop it into the bottle of vodka. Seal and let stand for 2 weeks.

Variation: To make Tangerine Vodka, substitute the zest from 2 tangerines or clementines for the lemon and crush it slightly before dropping into the vodka.

Mint Vodka

¼ cup fresh mint leaves
1 fifth (750 ml) vodka

Tie the mint leaves in rinsed, squeezed-dry cheese-cloth. Tie a long string onto the bundle. Drop the bundle into the vodka, letting the string hang out of the neck. Seal and let stand for 1 to 2 weeks, depending on the intensity of the flavor you want. Pull the mint out before serving the vodka.

Variation: To make Tarragon Vodka, simply substitute a 4-inch sprig of fresh tarragon for the mint leaves (you do not need to tie it in cheesecloth). This may not seem like enough, but it will flavor the vodka sufficiently.

Hot Pepper Vodka

1 hot fresh red or green chile pepper, or more
   to taste
1 fifth (750 ml) vodka

Drop the pepper into the vodka. Seal and let stand for a week. Taste, and decide whether the pepper should stay in longer, depending on the degree of "hotness" you want.

Left to right: Hot Pepper Vodka, Tarragon Vodka, Mint Vodka, Lemon Vodka

Apricot Liqueur

This deep-orange liqueur is marvelous alone as an after-dinner drink, and tasty splashed into a glass of champagne. Don't let the drained apricots go to waste—they can be spooned over vanilla ice cream for a potent dessert.

1 pound dried apricots, finely chopped
1 cup granulated sugar
1 fifth (750 ml) vodka, divided
3 tablespoons apricot brandy

In a small saucepan, combine the apricots, sugar, and 1 cup of the vodka. Bring just to a simmer over medium-low heat, stirring occasionally to dissolve the sugar. Remove from the heat and cool completely. Pour into a large glass jar and add the remaining vodka and apricot brandy. Cover tightly and let stand in a cool place for 2 months.

Pour the apricot mixture into a strainer set over a medium bowl. Let stand to drain well, at least 1 hour. (Some of the vodka will have soaked into the apricots.) Funnel the liqueur into an attractive bottle.

✖ *Makes about 1 pint*

Microwave Lemon Curd

The original inspiration for this recipe was handwritten in a worn old notebook covered in red oilcloth, which I inherited many years ago. "Mrs. Worship's Lemon Cheese," it read, in spidery black handwriting, under the date March 3, 1839. The quantities were sufficient to make five times this amount, in fifty times the time. But the principle is the same—and made in minutes in the microwave it is as special a treasure as you could wish to taste. This recipe was tested in a 700-watt microwave, so adjust timing to your oven's wattage.

8 tablespoons (1 stick) unsalted butter
3 large eggs
1 cup granulated sugar
Grated zest of 3 large lemons
½ cup fresh lemon juice

In a microwavable bowl, microwave the butter for about 3 minutes on High (100 percent power), until melted.

In a small microwave-proof bowl, whisk together the eggs, sugar, lemon zest, and juice until well combined. Whisk in the melted butter. Microwave on High (100 percent power) for 2 to 3 minutes, stirring often, until the curd is thick enough to coat a wooden spoon.

Remove from the microwave oven and pour into hot, sterilized jars. Cover and allow to cool at room temperature. Label "Keep Refrigerated," and mark with a "use-by" date of 4 weeks after the day the curd was prepared.

✄ *Makes about 2 cups*

Apricots and Prunes in Brandy

Do try this recipe. I am sure you will love it, and when you make it again, you may want to triple the quantities so that you will always have a good supply on hand, both for yourself and for gift giving. It goes quite magically with ice cream.

Try substituting port for the brandy. It produces an entirely different and very agreeable taste. For a bigger gift, put the fruit and brandy into a crystal bowl or a pottery crock, and include 2 antique-silver dessert spoons.

1 cup dried apricots (about 5 ounces)
1 cup pitted prunes (about 6 ounces)
1 cup granulated sugar
10 whole cloves
½ cup brandy, plus more, if needed

Place the apricots and prunes in separate bowls. Cover with cold water and allow to stand overnight.

Drain the apricots, reserving 1 cup of the liquid. Drain the prunes and discard the liquid.

Pour the reserved apricot liquid in a saucepan with the sugar and cloves. Heat over moderate heat until the sugar has dissolved. Increase the heat to high and boil the liquid until it has reduced to 1 cup. Pour in ½ cup of the brandy and remove from the heat.

Arrange the apricots and prunes in layers in hot, sterilized jars. Pour the syrup carefully into the jar, adding more brandy to cover, if needed, and attach the lids. Store for 3 weeks in a cool place before opening.

✄ *Makes 4 cups*

Microwave Lemon Curd, Apricots and Prunes in Brandy

Cookie Holly Wreath

Gingerbread Cookies

Lacy Chocolate Florentines

Lemon-Cardamom Wreaths

Molasses Crackles

Cinnamon Crisps

Chocolate-Orange Logs

Apple and Nut Pockets

Iced Ginger Stars

Jewel Biscotti

Cranberry-Oatmeal Crunchies

Puff Angels

Chapter Two

The Christmas Cookie Jar

Every December, home bakers around the world take out their most revered cookie recipes. Out come butter-stained newspaper clippings, chocolate-splattered recipe cards, and sugar-crusted stationery with the instructions for time-honored favorites. I hope that my offerings will be added to your collection of "must-have" holiday treats. (You will want to protect the pages of this book while cooking. My trick is to place a sheet of clear plastic wrap over the open pages as a splatter shield.)

I would like to offer a few tips on preparing perfect cookies:

These cookie recipes were tested with *bleached* all-purpose flour. Unbleached flour will make a tougher cookie.

If making your cookies in batches, place the dough on cool baking sheets. You may line the sheets for each batch with fresh aluminum foil so you don't have to wash and dry the sheets every time.

Position the oven racks in the top third and center of the oven. If the cookies are baked on the lower rack, they risk being burned on the bottom. Switch the positions of the sheets, from top to center and from center to top, halfway through the baking time for even browning.

If your dough should be refrigerated before rolling, chill it thoroughly, until firm. This will take at least 2 hours in most cases, but overnight is always best. You may place the dough in the freezer to shorten the chilling time if you wish. I rarely thoroughly freeze and defrost cookie dough, as the rising action can be affected.

Freeze baked cookies in airtight containers, separating the layers of cookies with waxed paper.

Cookie Holly Wreath

These tart, crisp cookies make a show-stopping centerpiece for a holiday buffet. If you can't find dried cranberries, cut glacé cherries into small rounds to simulate holly berries.

LEMON BUTTER COOKIES

8 tablespoons (1 stick) unsalted butter, softened
1 cup granulated sugar
2 large egg yolks
2 tablespoons water
1 tablespoon plus 1 teaspoon fresh lemon juice
Grated zest of 2 lemons
2 teaspoons vanilla extract
½ teaspoon salt
2 cups all-purpose flour

EGG "PAINT"

2 large egg yolks
¼ teaspoon green liquid food coloring

ICING

½ cup confectioners' sugar
1 tablespoon milk

4 ounces dried cranberries

To make the lemon butter cookies: Preheat the oven to 350° F. Lightly butter 2 baking sheets.

Using a hand-held electric mixer set at high speed, beat the butter and sugar together until light and creamy, about 2 minutes. Beat in the egg yolks, water, lemon juice, lemon zest, vanilla, and salt. Using a wooden spoon, work in the flour to form a soft dough. Gather up the dough into a thick disk, wrap in waxed paper, and refrigerate for at least 2 hours or overnight, until firm enough to roll out.

To make the egg "paint": Mix the egg yolks and food coloring until well combined.

On a lightly floured work surface, roll out half the dough ⅛ inch thick. If the dough is too firm, let it stand at room temperature until slightly softened. Using a 3-inch holly cookie cutter, cut out holly shapes. Gather up the scraps and reroll to cut out more cookies. Brush the tops of the cookies with the egg glaze. Place the cookies on the prepared sheets. To get a curved effect, place some of the glazed cookies, glaze side up, in a lightly buttered French bread (baguette) pan. Bake until the edges of the cookies are beginning to brown, 8 to 10 minutes. Immediately remove the cookies from the baking sheets and cool completely on wire cake racks.

To make the icing: Stir the confectioners' sugar and milk together until smooth. Using a dab of icing on each dried cranberry, place three berries in a cluster on the berry-shaped part of the cookie. (This is easiest to do if you place the icing in a pastry bag fitted with a small round decorating tip, such as Ateco Number 1.) Let the icing dry. (The cookies can be prepared up to 5 days ahead and stored at room temperature in an airtight container.)

To make the holly wreath: Arrange the cookies, ends overlapping, in a large circle on a large platter, decorated with a large bow. To hang the wreath, use the icing to glue the cookies onto a circle of strong cardboard. Attach a string to the back for hanging.
✄ *Makes 64 cookies*

Gingerbread Cookies

This mildly spiced dough makes soft, puffy cookie folk. If you like your gingerbread cookies thin and crispy, just roll out the dough to a ⅛-inch thickness.

GINGERBREAD COOKIES

8 tablespoons (1 stick) unsalted butter, softened
½ cup packed light-brown sugar
¾ cup unsulfured molasses
1 large egg
3 cups all-purpose flour
2 teaspoons ground ginger
1 teaspoon ground cinnamon
½ teaspoon ground cloves
½ teaspoon ground nutmeg
½ teaspoon baking soda
¼ teaspoon salt

PIPING ICING

2 cups confectioners' sugar
2 tablespoons half-and-half, approximately

Currants, raisins, candied fruits, candies, licorice strips, and colored sugars, for garnish

To make the gingerbread cookies: In a large bowl, using a hand-held electric mixer set at high speed, beat the butter until creamy, about 1 minute. Add the brown sugar and continue beating until light in color and texture, about 2 minutes. Beat in the molasses and egg. Sift together the flour, ginger, cinnamon, cloves, nutmeg, baking soda, and salt. Gradually work the flour mixture into the creamed mixture to form a soft dough. Scrape the dough onto a large piece of plastic wrap and wrap completely. Refrigerate until firm enough to roll out, at least 4 hours or preferably overnight.

Preheat the oven to 350° F. Lightly butter two baking sheets. On a well-floured surface, roll out half the dough to ¼ inch thickness. Using cookie cutters, cut out the cookies. Gather up the scraps of dough and work into the remaining dough. Repeat the process until all the dough is used. Place on the prepared baking sheets. Bake until just firm when pressed in the center with your finger, about 8 minutes. Cool for 2 minutes on the baking sheets, then transfer to wire cake racks to cool completely.

To make the piping icing: Stir the confectioners' sugar and half-and-half together in a small bowl. You may have to add more half-and-half by the teaspoon until you get an icing of piping consistency.

Transfer the icing to a pastry bag fitted with a small plain round tip, such as Ateco Number 4. Pipe the icing onto the cooled cookies, decorating as desired with the currants, raisins, candied fruit, candies, licorice strips, and colored sugars.

✕ *Makes about 16 5-inch-tall cookies*

Lacy Chocolate Florentines

Are they a brittle-like cookie, or a cookie-like confection? No matter—they are the height of elegance. Delicate almost to the point of transparency, florentines are a true test of your baking skills.

½ cup sugar
⅓ cup honey
⅓ cup heavy cream
1 cup finely chopped slivered almonds
½ cup finely chopped mixed candied peel
3 tablespoons all-purpose flour
3 tablespoons finely chopped raisins
Grated zest of 1 lemon
4 ounces bittersweet chocolate, finely chopped

Attach a candy thermometer to a medium saucepan. Add the sugar, honey, and cream and bring to a boil over medium heat, stirring constantly to dissolve the sugar. Cook until the thermometer reads 238° F., about 1 minute. Remove from the heat and stir in the almonds, candied peel, flour, raisins, and lemon zest. Set aside to cool.

Preheat the oven to 350° F. Line two baking sheets with parchment paper.

Place rounded teaspoons of the mixture at least 2 inches apart on the parchment paper. (The cookies will spread to be about 3 inches wide. Six cookies per baking sheet will usually be the maximum.) Using a fork dipped in cold water, press each mound of dough to form a round about 1½ inches in diameter.

Bake until the cookies are golden brown, 7 to 8 minutes. The cookies will be very soft, but will crisp upon standing. Let the cookies cool completely on the parchment paper. (You may slide the cookies, still on the parchment paper, off the sheet to cool so you can use the baking sheet for other batches.) Repeat the process until all the dough has been used.

Lift the cooled cookies off the parchment and place upside down on a waxed-paper–lined work surface. In the top part of a double boiler set over hot, not simmering, water, heat the chocolate, stirring occasionally, until melted. Remove from the water and let stand until tepid and slightly thickened, about 15 minutes.

Transfer the chocolate to a small, extra-strength plastic bag. Press all the chocolate into one corner, then snip off the end of the corner with scissors. Pipe thin lines of the chocolate in lacy patterns over the flat underside of the florentines. Cool until the chocolate is set. If your kitchen is warm, place the florentines, chocolate side up, on baking sheets, and refrigerate to set the chocolate. Store the florentines in an airtight container with waxed paper separating each layer.

Note: If you insist on having your cookies uniform, you may cut out exact rounds using a sharp 3-inch-round cookie cutter. Trim the cookies when they have cooled enough to be slightly firm, but still pliable.

✕ *Makes about 3 dozen cookies*

Clockwise from left: Cinnamon Crisps, Molasses Crackles, Apple and Nut Pockets, Lemon-Cardamom Wreaths, Lacy Chocolate Florentines

Lemon-Cardamom Wreaths

A Swedish friend sends me a box of these cookies every year, and I enjoy them so much that I begged for her recipe. She lines the dark wooden box with a beautiful napkin and arranges the cookies in rows. When I take the top off the box, the spicy smells of Christmas in the far north rise to greet me.

3½ tablespoons unsalted butter
1¼ cups all-purpose flour
⅔ cup superfine sugar
1 teaspoon vanilla extract
½ teaspoon ground cardamom
2 tablespoons grated lemon zest
1 large egg (approximately), lightly beaten

Measure the butter and flour into a large bowl. Using a pastry blender or 2 knives, mix well until crumbs are formed. Stir in the sugar, vanilla, cardamom, lemon zest, and sufficient egg to moisten. Knead together until smooth. Wrap in plastic wrap and refrigerate for several hours or overnight.

Preheat the oven to 400° F. Butter 2 baking sheets.

Divide the dough into 24 equal pieces. Roll each one into an 8-inch length. Place 2 lengths side by side and overlap them to form a double rope, then join the ends together to form a circle. Place on one of the prepared baking sheets. Repeat with the remaining pieces.

Bake in the preheated oven for 6 to 7 minutes, or until golden and firm. Transfer the wreaths to a wire rack and allow to cool.

✕ *Makes 12 wreaths*

Molasses Crackles

These crisp and crackly cookies, packed with spices, are made for dunking into a glass of cold milk. Whenever I smell these baking, I know Christmas has arrived.

1 cup sugar
¾ cup vegetable shortening
¼ cup unsulfured molasses
1 large egg
2 cups all-purpose flour
1 tablespoon ground ginger
2 teaspoons baking soda
1 teaspoon ground cinnamon
½ teaspoon salt
Sugar, for rolling

Preheat the oven to 350° F. Lightly butter 3 baking sheets. In a medium bowl, using a hand-held electric mixer set at high speed, beat the sugar and vegetable shortening until light in color and texture, about 2 minutes. Beat in the molasses and egg.

Sift together the flour, ginger, baking soda, cinnamon, and salt. A third at a time, add the flour mixture to the shortening mixture, beating until a soft dough has formed.

Lightly flour your hands. Break off level tablespoons of the dough and form into 1-inch balls. Roll the balls in sugar to coat. Place the coated balls of dough onto the baking sheets, allowing 2 inches between them.

Bake until the cookies are lightly browned, 12 to 15 minutes. Let cool on the baking sheets for a few minutes, then transfer to wire cake racks to cool completely.

✕ *Makes about 4 dozen*

Cinnamon Crisps

Every country makes its own distinctive Christmas cookies. These are the ones I remember from my British childhood. They were kept in a big "Toby" jar painted with a gaudy picture of King George V and Queen Mary, which lent a certain dignity to the cookies and encouraged us to eat them in small bites. This recipe is easily doubled.

8 tablespoons (1 stick) unsalted butter, softened
⅓ cup plus 1 tablespoon sugar
1 large egg yolk
½ teaspoon vanilla
1¼ cups all-purpose flour
1 teaspoon baking powder
1 teaspoon ground cinnamon
⅛ teaspoon salt
24 walnut halves

Preheat the oven to 375° F. Butter 2 baking sheets.

In a medium bowl, using a hand-held electric mixer set at high speed, beat the butter until creamy, about 1 minute. Add the sugar and continue beating until the mixture is light in color and texture, about 2 additional minutes. Beat in the yolk and vanilla.

Sift the flour, baking powder, cinnamon, and salt onto a sheet of waxed paper. Using a wooden spoon, work the dry ingredients into the creamed mixture to form a stiff dough. Scrape the dough onto another piece of waxed paper and form into a thick log about 8 inches long. Wrap the log in the waxed paper and refrigerate until chilled and firm, about 1 hour.

Using a sharp knife, cut the chilled dough into 24 slices, each about ⁵⁄₁₆ inch thick. Arrange the slices about 2 inches apart on the prepared baking sheets. Flatten the slices slightly with a fork, and top each with a walnut half.

Bake until golden brown, 10 to 12 minutes. Let cool on the baking sheets for 2 minutes, then transfer to wire cake racks to cool completely. The cookies will keep, stored in an airtight container at room temperature, for 3 days.

✖ *Makes 24 cookies*

Chocolate-Orange Logs

I adore the combination of chocolate and orange and like to add a little grated orange zest to hot chocolate, chocolate mousse—and, of course, chocolate cookies. This recipe has the added advantage that the plain cookies can be made ahead, then stored in the freezer for up to 3 months. Thaw them gradually for at least 3 hours before dipping them in melted chocolate.

2 cups all-purpose flour

⅛ teaspoon salt

2 tablespoons cornstarch

½ pound (2 sticks) unsalted butter

¼ cup confectioners' sugar

1 orange

4 ounces semisweet or milk chocolate, finely
 chopped

1 teaspoon vegetable shortening

Preheat the oven to 350°F.

Sift the flour, cornstarch, and salt onto a sheet of waxed paper.

Using a hand mixer set on high speed, cream the butter and sugar together in a medium-sized bowl until light and fluffy, about 2 minutes.

Grate the zest from the orange and add to the creamed mixture. Squeeze the juice and add 1 table-spoon of it to the mixture. Add the flour mixture and work it into the creamed mixture until a firm, smooth dough has formed, adding a little more orange juice if necessary to incorporate all the flour.

Spoon the mixture into a pastry bag fitted with a large open star tube (such as Ateco Number 6) and pipe 2-inch lengths onto ungreased baking sheets.

Bake in the preheated oven for 15 minutes, or until pale golden and firm.

Remove from the oven and allow the cookies to cool for 1 minute on the sheets before transferring them to a wire rack to cool completely.

Melt the chocolate and shortening in a bowl placed over a pan of very hot, not simmering, water, stirring occasionally until melted. Tilt the bowl so the melted chocolate collects in one corner. Dip an end of each cookie in the chocolate and place on waxed paper to dry.

The plain cookies can be stored in an airtight con-tainer for up to 2 weeks, but once dipped, they should be eaten within a couple of days.

✄ *Makes about 60 cookies*

Apple and Nut Pockets

These cookies are impressive in both size and flavor. Use store-bought apple butter or, for a real treat, homemade Golden Peach Butter (page 13).

DOUGH

8 tablespoons (1 stick) unsalted butter, softened
1¼ cups sugar
1 large egg
1½ teaspoons vanilla extract
2½ cups sifted all-purpose flour
½ teaspoon salt
¼ teaspoon baking soda

FILLING

⅔ cup apple butter
1 tablespoon lemon juice
Grated zest of 1 lemon
¼ cup finely chopped walnuts

Confectioners' sugar, for dusting

To make the dough: In a medium bowl, using a hand-held electric mixer set at high speed, beat the butter until creamy, about 1 minute. Add the sugar and beat until light in color and texture, about 2 minutes. Beat in the egg and vanilla.

Sift the flour with the salt and baking soda. Gradually add the flour mixture to the butter mixture, beating well after each addition.

Scrape the dough onto a large piece of plastic wrap and wrap tightly. Refrigerate until the dough is firm enough to roll out, at least 6 hours or preferably overnight.

To make the filling: Combine the apple butter, lemon juice, lemon zest, and walnuts and mix well.

Preheat the oven to 375° F. Divide the dough into 4 portions. On a lightly floured work surface, roll out one portion of dough to ⅛ inch thickness. (If the dough crumbles, work in your hands until malleable.) Using a 3-inch-round cookie cutter, cut out rounds of the dough. Gather up the scraps to work into the remaining dough. Repeat the process until all the dough has been used.

Place a rounded teaspoon of the filling in the center of half of the rounds. Brush the edges of the rounds lightly with water. Place the remaining rounds on top of the filled cookies. Using a fork, press the edges sealed. Don't worry if cracks appear in the surface. Transfer the cookies to ungreased baking sheets.

Bake until lightly browned, 12 to 15 minutes. Transfer to wire cake racks and cool completely. Sprinkle with confectioners' sugar before serving.

✘ *Makes about 20 large cookies*

Iced Ginger Stars

Ginger stars are traditional Christmas cookies that are handed down from parent to child. Recipes like this one should be counted among the family heirlooms.

GINGER STARS

5 cups all-purpose flour, plus a little extra,
   if the mixture is sticky
2 teaspoons baking soda
1 teaspoon ground ginger
1 teaspoon ground nutmeg
1 teaspoon salt
1 cup (2 sticks) unsalted butter, softened
1 cup packed dark-brown sugar
1 cup dark corn syrup
2 large eggs
2 teaspoons hot water
2 teaspoons lemon juice

GLACÉ FROSTING

1 cup confectioners' sugar, sifted
1 egg white, lightly beaten
1 teaspoon vanilla extract

To make the ginger stars: Sift the flour with the baking soda, ginger, nutmeg, and salt onto a sheet of waxed paper. In a large bowl, using a hand-held electric mixer set at high speed, beat the butter and brown sugar until light in color and texture, about 5 minutes. Beat in the corn syrup, eggs, hot water, and lemon juice until well blended.

Using a wooden spoon, gradually work in the sifted flour mixture until a firm dough has formed. If the mixture feels too sticky to handle easily, add a little more flour.

Divide the dough into 4 equal portions and wrap in plastic wrap. Refrigerate for at least 2 hours, until chilled and firm.

Preheat the oven to 350° F. Butter 4 baking sheets.

Lightly flour a work surface and rolling pin and roll out 1 of the pieces of dough until it is ⅛ inch thick. Using a star-shaped cookie cutter, cut out stars and transfer to the baking sheets and space 1 inch apart. (If you want to make cookies that will hang on the Christmas tree, place a small bean in each cookie. Remove after baking.) Bake for 10 to 12 minutes, or until the edges are light golden. While the cookies are baking, cut out more cookies.

Remove the baking tray from the oven and allow to stand for 1 minute while you bake the second tray of cookies. Using a thin metal spatula, transfer the cooled cookies to a wire rack to cool completely. Continue to roll, bake, and cool the remaining dough in the same way. Store the cooled cookies for up to 2 weeks in an airtight container.

To make the glacé frosting: Mix the sugar and egg white together in a small bowl. Stir in the extract and beat until a smooth icing has formed. Drizzle the frosting over the cookies. Allow to set before threading with a pretty narrow ribbon for hanging on the tree.

Variation: Use bought, ready-made icing and pipe different colored patterns on top of each star.

✖ *Makes about 128 2½-inch cookies*

Jewel Biscotti

A fancy form of everyday biscotti, all dressed up for Christmas. You may delete the glacé cherries and substitute an additional ½ cup chopped almonds.

2 cups sifted all-purpose flour
1 cup granulated sugar
1 teaspoon baking powder
3 large eggs
2 tablespoons kirsch
2 tablespoons Grand Marnier
1 teaspoon almond extract
½ cup chopped natural almonds
½ cup chopped glacé cherries

Preheat the oven to 300° F. Butter and flour a large baking sheet.

Mix the flour, sugar, and baking powder in a large bowl. In a small bowl, whisk together the eggs, kirsch, Grand Marnier, and almond extract. Add this mixture to the flour mixture. Stir in the almonds and cherries. Spoon the dough onto the prepared baking sheet and form it into a strip about 10 inches long, 5 inches wide, and ½ inch thick. Bake in the preheated oven for 45 minutes, or until set and firm to the touch. The dough shouldn't be hard.

Remove from the oven and slice diagonally with a serrated knife into ½-inch slices. (Discard the thick end pieces.) Arrange the slices on the baking sheet and return to the oven for 45 to 60 minutes, or until lightly brown.

Let the biscotti cool for about 5 minutes on the baking sheet, then transfer them to wire racks to cool completely. Store in an airtight container for up to 2 weeks.

✖ *Makes 20 cookies*

Cranberry-Oatmeal Crunchies

I am not going to pretend that cookies, even those made with oatmeal and cranberries, are particularly good for your body. I can say that they are very good indeed for your soul. Dried cranberries can be ordered from Williams-Sonoma, 1-800-541-2233, or substitute other dried fruits such as raisins.

1¼ cups (2½ sticks) unsalted butter
6 tablespoons light corn syrup
1⅓ cups packed light-brown sugar
2 cups rolled oats (old-fashioned, not "quick")
1⅓ cups dried cranberries
2 cups all-purpose flour
2 teaspoons baking soda
2 teaspoons hot water

Preheat the oven to 325° F. Butter 2 baking sheets.

Put the butter, syrup, and sugar into a small saucepan and heat gently over low heat until melted. Mix together the oats, cranberries, and flour, then stir into the melted mixture. Remove from the heat.

Mix together the baking soda and hot water in a small bowl and stir into the oat mixture. Allow to cool slightly. Using 1 level tablespoon for each, form the mixture into balls and place 2 inches apart on the baking sheets. Bake for 15 to 20 minutes, or until evenly browned.

Remove from the oven and allow to cool for 2 minutes before transferring the cookies with a metal spatula to a wire rack to cool completely. Continue baking with the remaining dough and cool baking sheets. When cool, store in an airtight container for up to 1 week.

✖ *Makes about 40 cookies*

Puff Angels

These puffy little angels are a heavenly mouthful of light flaky pastry encrusted with crisp caramelized sugar. They add a whimsical touch to the Christmas table, an angel placed at each setting.

1 17¾-ounce package frozen, all-butter puff
    pastry, defrosted
About ¾ cup sugar

On a lightly sugared work surface, unfold the puff pastry and sprinkle the surface with ¼ cup sugar. Using a rolling pin, gently press in the sugar without compressing the dough. Flip the dough and repeat on the other side.

Using a sharp knife, cut out a rectangle from the corner measuring 6 inches high and 8 inches wide. Cut it vertically down the center, and then cut each half into 10 rectangles measuring about 4 inches wide and 1¼ inches high. Place the little rectangles in the refrigerator and chill until firm, about 30 minutes. These will form the wings.

Line 2 heavy baking sheets with parchment paper and set aside. Using a 5-inch gingerbread-girl cutter, stamp out 9 cookies, pressing the cutter down firmly and evenly, cutting as close together as possible, and reversing the cookie cutter each time. Sprinkle each generously with more sugar. Arrange the cut pieces on the prepared trays, leaving as much space as possible between them. Prick each with a fork in about 6 places. Place the trays in the refrigerator and let them chill until firm, about 45 minutes.

Remove the small rectangles from the refrigerator and use a sharp chef's knife to slice each horizontally into 6 or 7 thin strips. Gather the strips in the center and pinch gently. Remove a tray from the refrigerator and place a bunch of dough strips under the upper body of each doughgirl, pressing firmly to adhere. Arrange the strips to point upward and use the knife to trim the ends so that they follow a line parallel to the tray edge.

Refrigerate the trays while the oven is preheating to 425° F. Sprinkle any remaining sugar over the dough. Bake for 15 minutes or until dark golden brown. Allow the cookies to cool on the paper before lifting them off.

✳ *Makes 9 cookies*

Cashew Nut Brittle

Hazelnut–Chocolate Toffee

Peanuty Rocky Road

Macadamia Nut Fudge

Candied Grapefruit Rinds

White Chocolate–Coconut Truffles

Dark Chocolate and Rum Truffles

Chocolate Lace Basket

Chapter Three

The Christmas Candy Dish

What better time to indulge in sweetmeats than during the holidays? Even if my candy dish is rarely overflowing during the year, December finds it brimming with toffee, brittle, and fudge.

If I had to give one tip about candymaking, it would be to buy a reliable candy thermometer. The best ones are attached to a metal plaque. Never rest the bulb of the thermometer on the bottom of the the saucepan, or you will get an inaccurate reading. Always be sure the thermometer is at least ½ inch from the bottom. Even the best thermometers can lose accuracy after a time. To check yours, attach it to a saucepan of briskly boiling water. If the thermometer reads 212° F. (or whatever your elevation's boiling point), all is well. If the reading is not exactly 212° F., make a note of the figure, and subtract or add the discrepancy to your temperatures when you use the thermometer. For ex-ample, if you got 215° F., your thermometer is 3 degrees over, so subtract 3 degrees from your temperature readings to get the true figure.

If a candy recipe says to cook without stirring, believe it! Stirring certain sugar syrups will cause sugar crystals to form, and the mixture will get grainy. You can wash off the sugar crystals that form on the insides of the pan with a clean, wet pastry brush. Press the wet brush on the sides of the pan while wiping, and the water will wash the sugar crystals into the syrup.

Most of these candies are perfect for sending as gifts. Place them in an airtight container in a larger box. Pour Styrofoam packing pellets or unshelled peanuts around the container to protect it from jostling during shipping. (Many people recommend using popped popcorn as the buffer, but insects can be attracted to the popcorn, so avoid it.)

Cashew Nut Brittle

Crunchy candies are always a great success. To prevent them from getting broken en route to a distant recipient, fill a large box with peanuts in their shells and nestle the tin of brittle in the center.

2 cups granulated sugar
1 cup light corn syrup
1 cup (2 sticks) unsalted butter
½ cup water
3 cups unsalted raw cashew nuts, coarsely chopped
2 teaspoons baking soda
1 teaspoon vanilla extract

Butter 2 baking sheets and set aside.

Butter the sides of a 3-quart saucepan, and add the sugar, corn syrup, butter, and water. Stir over low heat until the butter has melted. Increase the heat and bring the mixture to a boil. Continue cooking over moderate heat, without stirring, for about 20 minutes, until the temperature reaches 275° F. (soft-crack stage) on a candy thermometer.

Add the cashew nuts and continue cooking for about 5 minutes, until the candy thermometer registers 295° F. (hard-crack stage). You may stir occasionally, if necessary.

Remove from the heat and immediately sift the baking soda evenly over the surface. (Be careful—the syrup will foam up.) Add the vanilla and stir to distribute the soda and vanilla throughout the mixture.

Pour at once onto the prepared baking sheets. Tilt the sheets to spread the brittle about ½ inch thick. Allow to cool until firm.

Break the brittle into pieces and store in an airtight container.

Variation: Peanuts or other nuts can be added instead of the cashews, or you can use a combination of several nuts. Always choose the raw unsalted nuts that are available in health-food and specialty stores. The nuts will cook and "toast" when added to the hot syrup.

✖ *Makes about 2 pounds*

Hazelnut-Chocolate Toffee

Toffee is a thoughtful gift to give to any friend who has perfect teeth.

1¼ cups (2½ sticks) unsalted butter
1¼ cups packed light-brown sugar
¼ cup water
1 tablespoon honey
1 cup toasted and skinned hazelnuts, chopped
¼ teaspoon vanilla extract
1 cup semisweet chocolate chips (about 6 ounces)

Butter a small baking sheet.

Melt the butter over low heat in a large heavy saucepan. Add the sugar, water, and honey and stir constantly until melted, using a wooden spoon. Increase the heat to moderately high and continue cooking for 15 minutes, or until the mixture reaches 290° F. (hardball stage) on a candy thermometer, stirring often with a wooden spatula, scraping the bottom of the pan to make sure the mixture is not sticking.

Remove the pan from the heat and stir in the chopped nuts and vanilla extract. Pour the toffee evenly onto the prepared baking sheet. Cool about 5 minutes, until the surface is barely set. Sprinkle the top of the toffee with the chocolate chips. Let stand about 10 minutes, until the toffee is completely set and the chocolate is melted. Spread the chocolate evenly in a thin layer over the toffee. Cool completely until the chocolate is firm.

Break the toffee into rough pieces and store in an airtight container for up to 5 days.

✘ *Makes about 1 pound*

Clockwise from left: Candied Grapefruit Rinds, Hazelnut-Chocolate Toffee, Peanuty Rocky Road

Peanuty Rocky Road

Marshmallows, peanuts, and milk chocolate combine to make a quintessentially American confection. This recipe is easy to multiply out into big batches, so you can makes lots and cross many names off your gift list in one candymaking session.

1 pound milk chocolate, coarsely chopped
8 ounces large marshmallows, cut into quarters
1 cup unsalted roasted peanuts

In a heatproof bowl over hot, not simmering, water, heat the chocolate until almost completely melted. Remove from the water and let stand, stirring occasionally, until the residual heat melts the chocolate completely. Let the chocolate cool until tepid.

Lightly butter a baking sheet. Stir the marshmallows and peanuts into the tepid chocolate. (Stir a marshmallow into the chocolate as a temperature test. If it melts, the chocolate is still too warm; cool longer. If the chocolate stiffens, heat over hot water until the chocolate is softened.)

Spread onto the prepared baking sheet. Refrigerate until firm, at least 4 hours. Cut into pieces. (Store the rocky road at room temperature in an airtight container.)

✘ *Makes about 1¾ pounds*

Macadamia Nut Fudge

"Real" fudge (one that doesn't use marshmallows to ensure good results) is awfully difficult to make. This easy recipe is simply delicious, and can be made in about a third of the time of old-fashioned fudge, with no discernible loss of quality. I suggest wrapping small squares of the fudge in cellophane and tying the packets up in thin ribbon or gold cord. That way, the fudge parcels can double as Christmas-tree ornaments.

8 tablespoons (1 stick) unsalted butter, cut up

1 cup semisweet chocolate chips (about 6 ounces)

1 cup coarsely chopped macadamia nuts
     (about 4 ounces)

1 ounce unsweetened chocolate, finely chopped

1 teaspoon vanilla extract

2¼ cups sugar

1 5-ounce can evaporated milk

12 large marshmallows (about 3 ounces)

Butter an 8-inch-square baking pan. Line the bottom of the pan with foil.

In a large bowl, combine the butter, chocolate chips, macadamia nuts, unsweetened chocolate, and vanilla. Attach a candy thermometer to a medium saucepan. Add the sugar, evaporated milk, and marshmallows. Bring to a boil over medium heat, stirring constantly to prevent burning. Cook, stirring constantly, until the mixture reaches 238° F.

Pour the hot mixture into the bowl and let stand for 30 minutes. Stir until the mixture begins to thicken, about 1 minute. Spread evenly in the prepared pan. Let stand until completely cooled. Cover with foil and let stand overnight to allow the flavors to mellow.

Invert the fudge and remove the foil. Reinvert and cut into squares. Store the fudge at room temperature in an airtight container.

✖ *Makes about 2 pounds*

Candied Grapefruit Rinds, Macadamia Nut Fudge

Candied Grapefruit Rinds

I have to make several batches of these each Christmas because so many disappear as tasting samples that there are never enough to give as gifts. Fortunately, this recipe leaves you with extra syrup.

4 large thick-skinned pink grapefruit (the thicker the skin, the better the results)
4½ cups sugar
1½ cups water
Granulated sugar, for rolling the candied rinds

Using a sharp knife cut a thin slice off the tops and bottoms of each grapefruit. Cut away peel from the flesh in thick slices, reserving the grapefruit flesh for another use. Cut the peel into strips approximately 2 inches long and ½ inch wide.

Attach a candy thermometer to a large heavy saucepan, and add the sugar and water. Stir over medium-low heat just until the sugar has dissolved. Boil gently without stirring for 4 minutes, then add the grapefruit strips. Simmer slowly over very low heat for about 30 minutes, until the syrup reaches 240° F. on a candy thermometer. The rind will gradually become clear and transparent when it is fully cooked. Drain the strips, reserving the syrup if desired.

Lay a piece of waxed paper underneath a wire rack and, using tongs, arrange the strips on the rack. Leave until all the thick syrup has dripped away, at least 4 hours; preferably overnight. Put about a cup of granulated sugar onto another sheet of waxed paper and roll the strips, one at a time, in the sugar. Set the strips on a wire rack and leave to dry for about an hour.

When dry, pack the strips into jars with tight-fitting lids. They will keep in a cool place for at least 2 weeks. If they become slightly sticky, roll them again in granulated sugar.

Variations: Dip one end of each strip in melted dark chocolate and set on the rack to dry. Allow to harden completely before packing.

Candied thick-skinned orange rinds are made in the same way. This is a good use for the remaining syrup. To increase the quantity, add more water and sugar in the same proportions, three parts sugar to one part water.

Makes about 12 ounces

White Chocolate–Coconut Truffles

For recipes that use just a couple of tablespoons of liquor, you may not want to purchase a whole bottle. Many states sell tiny, individual serving-sized bottles of liquor, so search them out. Keep these truffles refrigerated until ready to serve.

4 tablespoons (½ stick) unsalted butter
8 ounces white chocolate, finely chopped
1 cup shredded sweetened coconut, divided
1 large egg yolk, at room temperature
2 tablespoons coconut liqueur or light rum
½ teaspoon vanilla extract

Melt the butter in a heatproof bowl over very hot, not simmering, water. Add the white chocolate and melt, stirring occasionally, just until smooth.

Remove from the heat and whisk in ¼ cup of the coconut, the egg yolk, coconut liqueur, and vanilla. The mixture may separate, but keep whisking and it will come together. Cover tightly with plastic wrap and refrigerate until firm, at least 3 hours or overnight.

Using a melon baller, scoop up the mixture and roll into 1-inch balls. Roll each ball in the remaining coconut, pressing the coconut on so it will adhere. Refrigerate until ready to serve. (The truffles can be prepared up to 3 days ahead, tightly covered and refrigerated, or frozen for up to 1 month.)

✖ *Makes about 30 truffles*

Dark Chocolate and Rum Truffles

May I suggest you consider putting just four scrumptious homemade truffles in a small porcelain box? An old friend did this for me one year and I admired both his taste and the taste of his homemade truffles enormously. Of course, you can use other combinations of nuts and liquors. Walnuts and cognac make glorious truffles, too.

8 ounces semisweet chocolate, finely chopped
3 tablespoons dark rum
1 teaspoon vanilla extract
6 tablespoons unsalted butter
½ cup confectioners' sugar
½ cup ground almonds
Unsweetened cocoa powder for coating

Melt the chocolate, rum, vanilla, and butter in a bowl set over a pan of hot, not boiling, water, stirring until completely incorporated. Remove from the heat, add the sugar and the ground almonds, and beat well. Cover tightly and refrigerate until firm, at least 4 hours or overnight.

Using a melon baller or a teaspoon, scoop up the mixture and roll into 1-inch balls. Toss in the cocoa powder and place in small foil candy cups. Refrigerate until ready to serve. (The truffles can be prepared up to 3 days ahead, tightly covered and refrigerated, or frozen for up to 1 month.)

✖ *Makes about 3 dozen truffles*

White Chocolate–Coconut Truffles in Chocolate Lace Basket

Chocolate Lace Basket

What a spectacular serving dish for your handmade truffles! Using chocolate-flavored confectioners' coating will ensure that your basket holds its shape. The coating is available in many supermarkets and candy supply shops, or by phone order from Maid of Scandinavia (1-800-328-6722). You can substitute 6 ounces (1 cup) semisweet chocolate chips melted with 1 teaspoon vegetable shortening for the confectioners' coating. However, if you use the chocolate chips to make your basket, refrigerate it until serving time and place it in a cool place during the party, or it may melt.

6 ounces chocolate-flavored confectioners' coating, finely chopped

Invert a round or oval shallow 1½-quart dish. Cover the *outside* of the bowl smoothly with aluminum foil. Freeze the covered bowl for 15 minutes.

Meanwhile, melt the coating in a heatproof bowl over hot, not simmering, water. Pour into the corner of a small, heavy-duty plastic food bag. Let cool until slightly thickened, about 15 minutes. Snip a ⅛-inch opening from the corner of the bag.

Reach up underneath and inside the inverted bowl with one hand so you can turn it easily while piping. Holding the bag a couple of inches above the bowl, and using small, tight spiral wrist movements, pipe a lacy pattern all over the foil-covered bowl. If the coating is the right temperature, it should flow from the bag without squeezing. Return the bowl to the freezer and let it chill until firm, about 15 minutes.

Carefully lift the foil from the bowl and place, right side up, onto a serving platter. Carefully peel off the foil. Place the truffles inside the lace basket, and serve immediately.

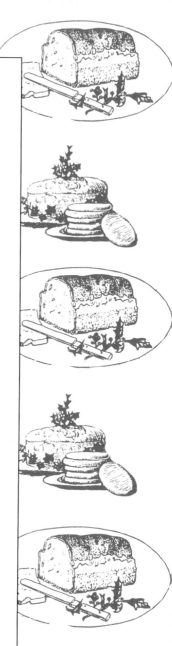

Pumpkin Muffins with Pumpkin Seeds

Pear and Walnut Bran Muffins

Breakfast Apple Bran Muffins

Orange Spice Muffins

Popovers with Bacon-and-Mushroom Stuffing

Cranberry-Walnut Streusel Bread

Sour Cream Coffee Cake with Chocolate and Walnuts

Cream Cheese and Raisin Wreath

Chapter Four

The Holiday Breakfast Table

A delicious breakfast is always a perfect way to start the day. During the holidays, with my home bursting with houseguests and friends "just dropping by for a quick cup of coffee and to say 'Merry Christmas,'" I like to have something warm out of the oven to share with my visitors. Fresh-baked bread simply tastes good enough without added incentive, but there is also the secondary benefit of filling the kitchen with toasty, spicy aromas.

Easy to make, and easier to eat, muffins are one of my favorite ways to fill up the breakfast breadbasket. I have all manner of muffins—pumpkin, apple-bran, pear-walnut, and orange-spice. In spite of the ingredients, all muffins have the same mixing procedure. Never overbeat muffin batter, and mix just until the ingredients are barely smooth. Overbeating causes tough muffins that will not rise nicely.

Light-as-air popovers are another quick addition to bolster the first meal of the day. While I like them plain or spread with a bit of jam, they are also fabulous edible baskets and can be stuffed with whatever pleases you. I suggest a bacon and mushroom mixture, but scrambled eggs and cheese or even ratatouille makes an excellent brunch entrée, too.

For fancier fare, try the Cranberry-Walnut Streusel Bread or Sour Cream Coffee Cake. Both of these quick breads can be baked the night before so all the cook has to do is slice them in the morning. If you are a yeast-dough fan, I have an excellent sweet bread that is a gorgeous centerpiece as well as delicious: Cream Cheese and Raisin Wreath.

Pumpkin Muffins with Pumpkin Seeds

The turkey people have persuaded us that turkey is not just for Thanksgiving—and now we are beginning to think that pumpkins, too, have a longer season than a single day of the year. These are nice and spicy and the seeds give them a good texture. They are at their best fresh from the oven.

2 cups all-purpose flour

¾ cup packed light-brown sugar

2 teaspoons baking powder

¼ teaspoon baking soda

½ teaspoon salt

1 teaspoon ground cinnamon

¼ teaspoon ground ginger

⅛ teaspoon ground cloves

¼ teaspoon ground nutmeg

1 cup canned pumpkin puree

4 tablespoons (½ stick) unsalted butter, melted
    and cooled

2 large eggs

¼ cup buttermilk

2 teaspoons vanilla extract

½ cup plus 2 tablespoons pumpkin seeds, coarsely
    chopped

Preheat the oven to 400° F. Butter 12 muffin cups.

Sift together the flour, sugar, baking powder, baking soda, salt, cinnamon, ginger, cloves, and nutmeg in a large bowl.

Combine the pumpkin, butter, eggs, buttermilk, and vanilla in another bowl. Make a well in the center of the dry ingredients, add the pumpkin mixture and stir just to combine. Stir in ½ cup of the pumpkin seeds. Spoon the mixture into the prepared muffin cups about three-fourths full, and sprinkle the remaining seeds on top of the muffins.

Bake in the preheated oven for 18 to 20 minutes, or until well risen and springy to the touch.

Allow the muffins to stand for 5 minutes before turning them out onto a wire rack to cool. Serve warm.
✖ *Makes 12 muffins*

Clockwise from left: Cream Cheese and Raisin Wreath, Popovers with Bacon-and-Mushroom Stuffing, Pear and Walnut Bran Muffins, Pumpkin Muffins with Pumpkin Seeds

Pear and Walnut Bran Muffins

This recipe and the one that follows ring the changes on our ever-present desire to be healthy through eating lots of bran. This one uses the real thing, not the packaged cereal.

1 large egg
1 cup buttermilk
¼ cup vegetable oil
1 cup wheat bran (available at natural-food stores)
⅓ cup dried pears, coarsely chopped
1 cup all-purpose flour
¼ cup packed light-brown sugar
1 teaspoon baking powder
½ teaspoon baking soda
¼ teaspoon salt
½ cup coarsely chopped walnuts
10 walnut halves, optional

Whisk together the egg, buttermilk, and oil in a large bowl. Stir in the bran and chopped pears. Allow to stand for 10 minutes.

Preheat the oven to 400° F. Butter 10 muffin cups.

Sift together the flour, sugar, baking powder, baking soda, and salt in a bowl. Fold this mixture into the buttermilk mixture until just moistened. Stir in the chopped walnuts, until just combined. Spoon the mixture into the prepared muffin cups about three-fourths full. Bake in the preheated oven for 18 to 20 minutes, or until well risen and springy to the touch. If desired, top the muffins with the walnut halves during the last 8 minutes of baking.

Allow the muffins to stand for 5 minutes before turning them out onto a wire rack to cool. Serve warm.
✗ *Makes 10 muffins*

Breakfast Apple Bran Muffins

1¼ cups all-purpose flour
2 teaspoons baking powder
¼ teaspoon salt
1½ cups bran-flake cereal
1¼ cups milk
¼ cup vegetable oil
¼ cup maple-flavored pancake syrup
1 large egg
1 Granny Smith apple, peeled, cored, and cut into 12 slices
1 tablespoon sugar

Preheat the oven to 400° F. Butter 12 muffin cups.

In a large bowl, mix together the flour, baking powder, salt, and bran-flake cereal.

In a small bowl, beat the milk, oil, maple-flavored syrup, and egg until well blended. Stir the egg mixture into the flour mixture until just combined. Spoon into the prepared muffin cups about three-fourths full. Place an apple slice on top of each muffin. Sprinkle with the sugar.

Bake in the preheated oven for 18 to 20 minutes, or until golden brown and springy to the touch.

Allow the muffins to stand for 5 minutes before turning them out onto a wire rack to cool. Serve warm.
✗ *Makes 12 muffins*

Clockwise from left: Sour Cream Coffee Cake with Chocolate and Walnuts, Orange Spice Muffins, Breakfast Apple Bran Muffins, Cranberry-Walnut Streusel Bread

Orange Spice Muffins

These will bring you nothing but praise.

1 cup all-purpose flour
1 cup whole-wheat flour
1 tablespoon baking powder
1¼ teaspoons ground cinnamon
¼ teaspoon ground cloves
¼ teaspoon ground nutmeg
¼ teaspoon salt
1 large egg
1 cup sour cream
4 tablespoons (½ stick) unsalted butter, melted
1 tablespoon frozen orange juice concentrate, thawed
Grated zest of 1 large orange
⅓ cup packed light-brown sugar
1 tablespoon sugar

Preheat the oven to 400° F. Butter 12 muffin cups.

Sift together the flours, baking powder, ¾ teaspoon of the cinnamon, the cloves, nutmeg, and salt.

In a separate bowl, beat the egg with the sour cream, butter, and orange juice. Stir in the orange zest and brown sugar and mix well.

Add the sour cream mixture to the dry ingredients and stir until just combined. Fill the prepared muffin cups about three-fourths full.

Combine the sugar with the remaining ½ teaspoon cinnamon and sprinkle over the muffins.

Bake in the preheated oven for 20 to 25 minutes, or until lightly browned and springy to the touch.

Allow the muffins to stand for 5 minutes before turning them out onto a wire rack to cool. Serve warm.

✗ *Makes 12 muffins*

Popovers with Bacon-and-Mushroom Stuffing

The response to fresh-out-of-the-oven popovers is similar to that brought on by being served a soufflé. This may be because, at their peak, both are like castles in the air, and there is no time to hang around admiring their architecture. They must be eaten at once while they are still hot properties.

You can, however, make the mushroom-and-bacon filling up to 1 hour in advance and set it aside at room temperature until you are just about ready to serve.

POPOVERS
2 tablespoons plus 1 teaspoon vegetable oil
1 cup all-purpose flour
1 cup milk
2 large eggs
¼ teaspoon salt

BACON AND MUSHROOMS
1 pound thick-sliced bacon, cut into 1-inch pieces
4 tablespoons (½ stick) unsalted butter
3 small onions, finely chopped
1 pound white button mushrooms, thinly sliced
½ pound fresh shiitake mushrooms, stems removed, caps thinly sliced

To make the popovers: Preheat the oven to 450° F. Put ½ teaspoon of vegetable oil in each of 8 sections of a muffin tin. Put the tin in the oven and heat until very hot, 3 to 5 minutes.

Meanwhile, put the flour, milk, eggs, salt, and the remaining 1 tablespoon of oil in a blender or food processor. Blend at high speed for 20 seconds, or until the batter is smooth. Turn the blender off, scrape the sides of the jar down with a rubber spatula, and blend again for a few seconds.

Remove the muffin tin from the oven. Pour the batter into the hot cups, filling them about half full. Bake until crisp and well browned, 25 to 30 minutes. Remove the popovers from the tin and wrap in a clean kitchen towel to keep warm until ready to serve.

To make the bacon-and-mushroom filling: Cook the bacon over medium-high heat in a large heavy skillet until crisp, about 5 minutes. Remove the bacon with a slotted spoon and drain on paper towels. Discard the bacon fat.

Add the butter and onions to the skillet and cook over medium-high heat, stirring, until softened but not browned, about 5 minutes. Add the white and shiitake mushrooms and cook until tender, about 8 minutes.

Just before you are ready to serve, toss the reserved crisp bacon with the mushrooms and onions in the skillet. Cook, stirring, over moderate heat just until heated through.

Make a well in the center of each popover and fill with the hot bacon-and-mushroom mixture. Transfer the filled popovers to a warmed serving platter and serve immediately.

✕ *Serves 8*

Cranberry-Walnut Streusel Bread

Tangy cranberries are cloaked in a spiced quick bread to make a delectable breakfast treat. This bread would be equally popular at teatime. As the recipe is easily doubled, you may want to make two loaves, and either give one as a gift or freeze for future enjoyment.

CRANBERRY BREAD

1½ cups all-purpose flour
1 teaspoon baking soda
1 teaspoon baking powder
1 teaspoon ground cinnamon
½ teaspoon salt
1 cup sugar
2 tablespoons (¼ stick) unsalted butter, melted
2 large eggs
Grated zest of 1 orange
½ cup orange juice
1 cup fresh or frozen cranberries
½ cup coarsely chopped walnuts
½ cup golden raisins

STREUSEL

¼ cup flour
2 tablespoons sugar
2 tablespoons (¼ stick) unsalted butter, softened

Preheat the oven to 350° F. Butter and flour a 9- by 5-inch loaf pan.

To make the cranberry bread: Sift together the flour, baking soda, baking powder, cinnamon, and salt. In a large bowl, using a hand-held electric mixer set at medium speed, beat the sugar, melted butter, eggs, and orange zest until combined. Alternately in thirds, beat in the flour mixture and the orange juice, scraping the sides of the bowl as needed. Stir in the cranberries, walnuts, and raisins. Transfer to the prepared pan.

To make the streusel: Work the flour, sugar, and butter with your fingers in a small bowl until it forms large crumbs. Sprinkle the crumbs evenly over the top of the bread.

Bake until a toothpick inserted in the center of the loaf comes out clean, about 1 hour 15 minutes. (The streusel will sink into the bread as it bakes.) Cool the bread in the pan for 10 minutes, then turn out onto a wire cake rack to cool completely.

Makes 1 loaf

Sour Cream Coffee Cake with Chocolate and Walnuts

This is my favorite coffee-cake recipe. I have read in other books that people freeze coffee cakes. I don't. I think it spoils them, and besides, there is never enough left to think about doing any such thing.

1 cup (2 sticks) unsalted butter, softened

¾ cup sugar

2 cups sifted all-purpose flour

¼ teaspoon salt

1 teaspoon baking soda

2 teaspoons baking powder

3 large eggs

1 cup sour cream

2 teaspoons vanilla extract

1 cup coarsely chopped walnuts

4 ounces bittersweet chocolate, coarsely chopped

Preheat oven to 350° F. Butter and flour a 10- to 12-cup fluted tube pan.

In a large bowl, using a hand-held electric mixer set at high speed, beat the butter until creamy, about 1 minute. Add the sugar and continue beating at high speed until light and creamy, about 2 minutes.

Sift together the flour, salt, baking soda, and baking powder. At low speed, beat in ½ cup of the flour mixture, then beat in 1 of the eggs. Beat in another ½ cup of the flour mixture, then 1 of the remaining eggs. Repeat with another ½ cup of the flour mixture, and the last egg. Beat in the remaining flour along with the sour cream and vanilla. Using a spatula, fold in the walnuts and chocolate. Transfer the batter to the prepared pan and smooth the surface.

Bake for 45 to 55 minutes in the preheated oven until the cake begins to shrink from the sides of the pan and a toothpick inserted in the center comes out clean. The surface will crack.

Remove the cake from the oven and let it cool for about 10 minutes in the pan, then turn it out onto a wire cake rack. Cool completely before serving.

✂ *Serves 12*

Cream Cheese and Raisin Wreath

This is a fancier version of cheese Danish, a beautiful bread to place on your breakfast table. If you like, make the dough the night before, place a heavy plate on top to stop the dough from overrising, and refrigerate to slow the fermentation of the yeast. In the morning, your dough will be ready to complete the wreath.

SWEET DOUGH

3 cups all-purpose flour
6 tablespoons sugar
2 packages (2¼ teaspoons each) active dry yeast
½ teaspoon ground cardamom
¼ teaspoon salt
6 tablespoons (¾ stick) unsalted butter, cut into pieces
⅓ cup water
⅓ cup milk
1 large egg

CREAM CHEESE FILLING

3 ounces cream cheese
1 large egg
4 tablespoons sugar
¼ cup golden raisins
½ teaspoon vanilla extract

DRIZZLE ICING

½ cup confectioners' sugar, sifted
¼ teaspoon vanilla extract
2 to 3 teaspoons lemon juice

To make the dough: In a large bowl, whisk 1 cup flour, and the sugar, yeast, cardamom, and salt to combine. In a small saucepan, heat the butter, water, and milk over very low heat just until very warm, about 100° F. The butter does not have to melt completely. Using a hand-held electric mixer set at medium speed, gradually fold the liquids into the flour mixture and beat for 2 minutes. Add the egg and ½ cup of flour and beat for 2 minutes at high speed, scraping the bowl occasionally. Using a wooden spoon, gradually work in the remaining flour to form a soft dough. (You may have to add more flour.) Transfer the dough to a buttered bowl and turn to coat the dough. Cover tightly with plastic wrap and let rise in a warm, draft-free place until doubled in bulk, 50 to 60 minutes.

To make the filling: In a small bowl, beat the cream cheese until fluffy. Beat in the egg, sugar, raisins, and vanilla.

Punch down the dough and turn out onto a lightly floured surface. Roll the dough into a 16-inch circle. Drape the circle over a buttered 6-cup ring mold. Gently fit the dough into the mold, leaving about a 1-inch overhang. Let the dough cover the center opening of the ring.

Spoon the cream-cheese filling into the mold. Fold the overhang back over the filling, seal the edges where they meet the inside ridge of the ring. Using scissors, cut a cross in the dough extending over the center ring to form 4 triangles. Fold each triangle back over the dough. Cover with plastic wrap and let rise in a warm place until double in bulk, about 50 minutes.

Preheat the oven to 350° F. Bake until a toothpick inserted in the center comes out clean and the wreath is golden brown, about 30 minutes. Invert the wreath

onto a plate, then reinvert onto a wire cake rack to cool until warm.

To make the icing: Combine the confectioners' sugar and vanilla in a small bowl. Gradually stir in enough lemon juice to make a glaze of drizzling consistency.

Transfer the icing to a small heavy-duty plastic bag and squeeze into one corner of the bag. Using scissors, snip a small opening from the corner. Pipe the icing over the wreath. Serve the wreath warm or at room temperature.

✕ *Makes 8 to 10 servings*

No-Bake Christmas Cookie House

Chocolate Yule Log (Bûche de Noël)

Candied Caramel Apples

Chocolate Cookie Tree

Gingerbread House

Popcorn Snowmen

Salt-Dough Christmas Ornaments

Chapter Five

Fun Kitchen Projects for the Whole Family

I firmly believe that children should get into the kitchen at the earliest possible age. It is so important to teach them about the taste of freshly prepared food, and while cooking, they will soak up lots of information about mathematics and cleanliness. Most of all, cooking is fun.

These projects are designed with the whole family in mind. Certainly an adult will want to be present to supervise the nuts and bolts of the operation, but once everything is set up, you can let the kids' creativity take over. For the younger set, I recommend that an adult accurately measure the ingredients and set them out. After that crucial step is completed, allow the children to mix to their hearts' content.

If food coloring is involved, either in painting projects or in the frosting, cover the table with an inexpensive plastic tablecloth, or even plastic wrap. Be sure everyone is wearing old clothes to avoid anxiety over paint stains.

No-Bake Christmas Cookie House

Kids love this project because they can start assembling right away—no need to wait for cookies to bake and cool. An empty tissue box is used as a frame for the house, making it sturdy and durable.

....

Decorating Icing

4½ cups (1 pound) confectioners' sugar
3 large egg whites

EQUIPMENT
Pastry bag fitted with Ateco Number 6 tip, or
    Ziploc bags
1 empty tall tissue box (5½ inches tall by 4½
    inches wide)
Cardboard base
Graham crackers
Shredded coconut
Red and green sprinkles
Peppermint candies
Mini-marshmallows
Red and green candied fruit strips
Chocolate licorice
1 vanilla wafer

To make the decorating icing: In a large bowl, stir together the confectioners' sugar and the egg whites. With a hand-held electric mixer, set at high speed, beat until the mixture is stiff and firm, about 5 minutes. Fill a pastry bag fitted with a plain round decorating tip, such as Ateco Number 6, with the icing; alternately, use a Ziploc bag—fill with the icing, seal, and snip the bottom corner of the bag to make a ¼-inch hole.

Lay the tissue box on its side on the cardboard base so that the opening of the tissue box will be the door opening for the house. With a sharp knife, score 9 whole graham crackers along the perforated lines and gently break them into quarters to make "bricks." Score and gently break three quarters in half crosswise to make smaller bricks. Using the decorating icing as glue, cover the sides and back of the house as shown in the diagram. Pipe a line of icing at each corner seam to reinforce the house.

To create the roof, pipe a thick line of icing down the center of the top of the tissue box. Stand 1 whole graham cracker in the icing to make a 5-inch-long, 2½-inch-high center beam. Pipe the icing along the bottom of both sides of the cracker to reinforce it. Allow the icing to harden completely. To attach the roof pieces, pipe a thick line of icing on the top edge of the center beam and along the top edge of both sides of the house. Use 2½ whole graham crackers on each side as roof pieces; press into place. Pipe a line of icing along the peak of the roof where the crackers meet. Allow the icing to harden completely. To fill in the space below the roof peak at the front and back ends of the house, fit ½ of a graham cracker into the peak at each end so they appear diamond-shaped; trim the bottom points so they are even with the top of the walls; attach to the roof with icing.

With a metal icing spatula, spread a thick layer of icing over both sides of the roof, covering the graham crackers completely. Scatter the coconut on the roof, then, the red and green sprinkles. Pipe a line of icing along the bottom and side edges of the roof and randomly pull the tip of pastry bag down through the icing to make "icicles."

To make the chimney, stack three peppermint candies, with icing between them; attach to the rear end of the roof with a generous dab of icing.

To make the windows on the sides of the house, pipe a 1½-inch-wide circle in the center of each side; attach the ends of mini-marshmallows to the circle, filling in the circle of icing completely.

To decorate the front of the house, first cover the tissue-box opening with graham-cracker quarters as shown in the diagram. Then cover the front of the house, below the diamond-shaped roof piece, with ic-ing. Attach a row of peppermint candies, and cut pieces of candied fruit strips, as pictured. Use cut pieces of chocolate licorice to frame the doorway. If desired, attach one vanilla wafer to the bottom of the door to make front step. Allow the icing to harden completely before transporting the house.

✕ *Makes 1 Cookie House*

Chocolate Yule Log (Bûche de Noël)

⅔ cup unsifted all-purpose flour
3 tablespoons unsweetened cocoa powder
½ teaspoon baking powder
¼ teaspoon salt
3 large eggs, at room temperature
¾ cup superfine sugar
¼ cup water
1 teaspoon vanilla
4 tablespoons confectioners' sugar
1 cup heavy cream

....

Fudge Frosting

1 cup heavy cream
8 ounces semisweet chocolate finely chopped
8 ounces dried apples
Spearmint candy leaves
6 mini-marshmallows, optional
Ground cinnamon, optional

Line a 15½- by 10½-inch jelly-roll pan with waxed paper or aluminum foil; grease. In a medium-sized bowl, mix the flour, cocoa, baking powder, and salt and set aside.

Heat the oven to 375° F. In a large bowl, use a hand-held electric mixer set at high speed, beat the eggs until very thick and pale yellow—about 4 to 5 minutes. Beat in the water and vanilla on low speed. Gradually fold in the flour mixture, blending until the batter is smooth. Pour the batter into the pan and spread evenly to the corners. Bake 12 to 15 minutes or until a cake tester inserted in the center comes out clean. Loosen the cake from the edges of the pan.

Sprinkle 2 tablespoons of the confectioners' sugar over a clean dishcloth; invert the cake onto the cloth. Carefully remove the waxed paper or foil. While still hot, roll the cake with the towel from the narrow end; cool completely.

To prepare the fudge frosting: In a small saucepan, heat the heavy cream to boiling; remove from heat and add the chocolate. Gently stir the chocolate and cream until all of the chocolate is melted and the mixture is smooth. Allow to cool until thickened to frosting consistency. (If desired, refrigerate the mixture briefly to hasten cooling; check frequently as the frosting will become very firm with chilling.) Makes 2 cups.

To assemble the cake: Beat the cream with 1 tablespoon of the confectioners' sugar until stiff. Gently unroll the cake and remove the towel. Spread the whipped cream evenly over the cake. Roll up the cake with the cream; spread the fudge frosting over the sides and ends of the cake. With the tines of a fork, make strokes in the frosting to resemble a tree trunk. Decorate with rows of apple chips to resemble bark; place spearmint leaves on the log. Sift the remaining 1 tablespoon confectioners' sugar over the log to create a snow effect.

If desired, make marshmallow mushrooms: Flatten 3 mini-marshmallows with a rolling pin to make round mushroom "tops." With a small dab of frosting, attach the tops to the short ends of the remaining 3 marshmallows; dust the tops of the mushrooms with cinnamon and stand them in place on the log.

✖ *Makes 6 to 8 servings*

Candied Caramel Apples

Caramel, white chocolate, pistachios, and candy Red Hots transform the simple apple into something spectacular—a kind of Cinderella recipe.

8 small apples
8 wooden sticks
1 14-ounce package Kraft caramels
2 tablespoons water
1-inch-thick Styrofoam board, optional
3 ounces white chocolate, finely chopped
Pastry bag fitted with an Ateco Number 1 tip,
    or Ziploc bags
¼ cup coarsely chopped natural pistachios
16 Red Hots candy, cut in half with a large sharp
    knife

Wash and dry the apples; insert a stick into the stem end of each apple. In a heavy, 1½-quart saucepan over low heat, melt the caramels with the water, stirring frequently until smooth. Dip the top half of each apple into the melted caramel, turning to coat. Stand the caramel-coated apples upright by inserting the sticks into the Styrofoam board; set aside. (If Styrofoam is not available, place the apples on lightly greased waxed paper; set aside.)

In the top of a double boiler set over gently simmering water, melt the white chocolate, stirring frequently. When the white chocolate is smooth, transfer to the pastry bag fitted with an Ateco Number 1 tip, or a Ziploc bag with one bottom corner snipped to make a very small hole—about ⅛ inch wide.

Randomly drizzle white chocolate over the caramel apples. Press the chopped pistachio pieces into the caramel and decorate each apple with 4 half-pieces of Red Hots candy. Serve immediately or store in the refrigerator. If chilled, let stand at room temperature 15 minutes before serving to allow the caramel to soften.
✗ *Makes eight small candied apples*

Chocolate Cookie Tree

The cookie dough for this creation needs to chill at least two hours—overnight is even better.

CHOCOLATE COOKIE DOUGH

1¼ cups confectioners' sugar

8 tablespoons (1 stick) unsalted butter, softened

1 large egg

1 teaspoon vanilla extract

1¼ cups all-purpose flour

3 tablespoons unsweetened cocoa powder

¼ teaspoon salt

⅛ teaspoon baking soda

DECORATING ICING

4½ cups confectioners' sugar (about 1 pound)

3 large egg whites

FOR ASSEMBLING AND DECORATING

1 large Christmas-tree cookie cutter (see Note)

Pastry decorating bag with Ateco Number 6 tip, or
    Ziploc bags

Cardboard base

Jelly beans or gum drops

Red and green candied fruit strips

Cotton balls

Rock candy, optional

To make the chocolate cookie dough: In a large bowl with an electric mixer, beat together the sugar and butter until light in color and texture. Add the egg and vanilla; beat until the mixture is well blended and smooth. Sift the flour, cocoa, salt, and baking soda into the butter mixture; mix, by hand, until a smooth dough forms. Divide the dough into thirds (dough will be slightly sticky), wrap in plastic, and refrigerate at least 2 hours or overnight.

To make the pieces for the chocolate cookie tree: Heat the oven to 375° F. Lightly dust with flour an ungreased cookie sheet or the back of an ungreased jelly-roll pan. Roll out one piece of dough to a ¼-inch-thick triangle, measuring about 10 inches vertically and about 9 inches wide at its base. Place the cookie cutter on top of the triangle and press to make the tree; remove the excess dough and run a knife around the cutter to make a clean edge. Remove the cutter and bake the cookie tree 10 to 12 minutes or until the edges brown slightly. Immediately run a long spatula under the tree to prevent sticking. Let cool 5 minutes on the cookie sheet; transfer to a wire rack and cool completely.

With the remaining dough make two more cookie trees as above, but immediately after baking, while the cookies are hot, cut a ¼-inch-wide strip out of each cookie, from the top of the tree to the bottom, creating two halves from each cookie. Run the spatula underneath the halves, cool a few minutes on the cookie sheet, then transfer to a wire rack and cool completely.

To make the decorating icing: In a large bowl, stir together the confectioners' sugar and the egg whites. With an electric mixer, beat at high speed for 5 minutes or until the mixture is stiff and firm. Fit a pastry bag with an Ateco Number 6 tip and fill with icing; alternately, use a Ziploc bag—fill with icing, seal, and snip one bottom corner of the bag to make a ¼-inch hole. (Tightly cover the remaining icing, as it dries out quickly.)

To assemble and decorate the cookie tree: Pipe a thick line of icing on the bottom edge of the whole cookie tree; stand the tree on the cardboard base, and pipe thick lines of icing on both sides of the bottom

of the tree to secure it to the base. Hold in place several minutes if necessary; allow the icing to harden completely.

On one side of the whole cookie, join two of the cookie halves to the center of the whole cookie with a thick line of icing; fan the halves to make three equal spaces between the pieces. Reinforce all the joints with icing. Repeat on the other side of the whole cookie with the remaining halves to complete the tree. Allow the icing to set and harden completely.

To decorate the tree, pipe lines of icing along the outside edges of the tree; stud them with jelly beans or gum drops.

Make bows with candied fruit strips: Cut an 8-inch piece of red or green candied fruit strip. Cross the ends, creating a loop with 1 inch of each end extending; pinch the loop at the center to meet where the ends cross, creating a bow. Wrap a contrasting-colored candied fruit strip around the center of the bow to keep it intact. Repeat to make 8 bows. Attach one bow to each section of the tree with a dab of icing; attach two bows to the top of the tree.

To cover the cardboard base with "snow," spread a thin layer of icing over the base. Attach cotton balls all over and scatter rock candy, if desired.

Note: Wilton Enterprises, Inc., makes the giant Christmas-tree cookie cutter used in this recipe. It can be found in most cookware shops or mail-ordered from the company. For information, write Wilton Enterprises, Inc., 2240 West 75th Street, Woodbridge, Illinois 60517. Or, call 708 963-7100.

Makes one tree

Gingerbread House

Though it's still an all-afternoon project to create a candy-studded colorful gingerbread house, the method used here is easy and foolproof. Using a standard-size shoebox to make the patterns for the sides, roof, and ends of the house, many of the measurements and straight sides already exist.

GINGERBREAD DOUGH

2½ cups all-purpose flour

1 teaspoon ground cinnamon

1 teaspoon ground ginger

¼ teaspoon ground cloves

¼ teaspoon baking soda

¼ teaspoon salt

½ cup vegetable shortening

½ cup sugar

¼ cup unsulfured molasses

1 large egg

DECORATING ICING

4½ cups confectioners' sugar (about 1 pound)

3 large egg whites

FOR ASSEMBLING AND DECORATING

11- by 5-inch shoebox

Pastry decorating bag with Ateco Number 6 tip,
 or Ziploc bags

Cardboard base

Shredded-wheat biscuits

Jelly beans

Green food coloring

Sugar cone

Multicolored sprinkles

Cotton balls or wads of cotton

To prepare the gingerbread dough: In a medium bowl, sift together the flour, cinnamon, ginger, cloves, baking soda, and salt. Set aside. In a large bowl with an electric mixer at high speed, beat together the vegetable shortening and sugar for 3 minutes. Scrape down the sides, add the molasses and egg and beat 3 minutes or until the mixture is well blended and smooth. Add the flour mixture and stir, by hand, to form smooth dough. Divide the dough in half, wrap each half in plastic, and refrigerate at least 1 hour or overnight.

Meanwhile, make 3 patterns for the house—one side, one end, and one roof pattern, following the instructions on page 85.

To make the parts of the house (one front end, one back end, two sides, two roof pieces): Heat the oven to 350° F. Lightly dust with flour an ungreased cookie sheet or the back of an ungreased jelly-roll pan. Roll out one ball of dough to ⅛ inch thick. Lay out the cardboard patterns (as many as will fit), leaving one inch between them. With a knife, cut around each one, removing the excess dough. (Form the dough scraps into a ball and reserve.) Run the knife around each piece a second time to clean up ragged edges. Remove the patterns and bake the gingerbread pieces 15 to 18 minutes or until the edges brown slightly. Immediately run a long spatula under each piece to prevent sticking. Let cool 5 minutes on a cookie sheet; carefully transfer to a wire rack and cool completely. Roll, cut, and bake the remaining half of the dough and all the dough scraps to complete all 6 pieces of the gingerbread house.

To prepare the decorating icing (when you are ready to assemble the gingerbread house): In a large bowl, stir together the confectioners' sugar and egg whites. With an electric mixer, beat at high speed 5 minutes

or until the mixture is stiff and firm. Fit a pastry bag with an Ateco Number 6 tip and fill with icing; alternately, you can use a Ziploc bag—fill with icing, seal, and snip one bottom corner of the bag to make a ¼-inch hole. (Tightly cover the remaining icing, as it dries out quickly.)

To assemble and decorate the gingerbread house: Decorate the front end piece and two side pieces of the house as shown or as desired, using icing as glue for ornaments. Let dry completely.

To put the house together, pipe a thick line of icing along the bottom edge of the back end piece; pipe a thick line of icing on the bottom and back edges of one side piece. Stand and join the back end and the side on the cardboard base, holding in place several minutes to allow the icing to dry slightly. (You can also use tall round glasses to help keep the pieces in place while drying.) Reinforce the house by piping icing along the inside joint.

Pipe icing on the bottom and back edges of the second side piece; press into place and reinforce the inside joint.

Pipe icing on the bottom edge and the side edges of the front piece; press into place and reinforce. Let the icing set.

To put the roof on, pipe icing along all the top edges; press the roof pieces into place and hold for several minutes while the icing sets. Let the icing set completely.

Attach the shredded-wheat biscuits to create a "thatched" look: With a long knife, gently split each biscuit to create two halves. Pipe two thick rows of icing on the inside of each biscuit half; press the halves into place on the bottom of one roof side to create a row of "thatch." Repeat splitting and icing to create a top row of "thatch." Repeat to cover the other side of the roof. To fill in any bare spots on the roof, split biscuits and cut to size; ice and press to roof. Decorate the front edge of the roof with a thick line of icing studded with jelly beans. Make "icicles" on the bottom edges of the roof by piping large dots of icing and pulling the pastry tip downward.

Make a chimney on the back end of the roof, using jelly beans, stacked bricklike, in a square.

To make a Christmas tree for the front of the house: Mix ½ cup decorating icing with several drops of green food coloring and blend to make dark-green icing. Cover the sugar cone with a thick layer of green icing; to create an evergreen effect, use a small paring knife to randomly "pull" the icing out from the cone. Decorate the tree with multicolored sprinkles and attach it to the cardboard base in front of the house using icing.

To cover the cardboard base with "snow," spread a thin layer of icing over the base. Arrange torn cotton balls or wads randomly to create a snow effect.

✖ *Makes 1 gingerbread house*

GINGERBREAD PIECES FROM A SHOEBOX

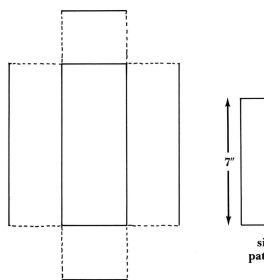

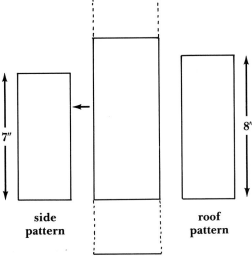

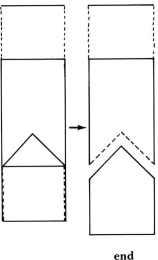

Cut all the corners of the shoebox so it lies flat.

From the side pieces of the box cut one piece 7 inches long for the side of the house; one piece 8 inches long for the roof.

To make the end pattern, fold in one bottom end to lie on top of the box bottom; draw a line across. Mark a point 2 inches up from the center of the line. Connect the point to the ends of the line creating a triangle. Cut out a triangle-topped square.

Popcorn Snowmen

This kitchen project creates a sextet of jaunty popcorn snow-men that are as much fun to make as they are to eat. To get 9 cups of popped corn, you will need about 1⅓ cups raw popcorn.

4 tablespoons (½ stick) unsalted butter
4 cups mini marshmallows
9 cups popped popcorn
½ cup confectioners' sugar
1 tablespoon milk
Gumdrops, cinnamon candies, fruit leather, jelly
    beans, for garnish

In a large saucepan, melt the butter over low heat. Add the marshmallows and cook, stirring often, until melted and syrupy, about 5 minutes.

Place the popped popcorn in a large lightly greased shallow pan. Pour the syrup over the popcorn, tossing to coat evenly. While still warm, form 6 balls about 5 inches in diameter from the coated popcorn for the bottom sections, giving the balls flat bases so the snow-men will stand. Form 6 balls about 3½ inches in diameter for the middle sections. Then form 6 balls about 2 inches in diameter for the top sections.

Stir the confectioners' sugar and milk together until smooth. Use the icing to stack three popcorn balls of decreasing sizes into a snowman, then attach candies to decorate.

✘ *Makes 6 snowmen*

Salt-Dough Christmas Ornaments

A high concentration of salt in this dough makes these ornaments inedible but prevents spoilage. And with a coat of clear shellac or varnish on each painted piece, these creations can be preserved for years.

The designs below are especially suited to young hands but in this project anything goes—let your imagination loose. Experiment with kitchen tools or household items such as a fork, pocket comb, hand-held grater, bottle cap, and pastry cutter, to get different effects. Or use cookie cutters you have on hand and add little embellishments.

SALT DOUGH

3 cups all-purpose flour

1½ cups table salt

¾ to 1 cup water

EQUIPMENT

Flour

Ungreased cookie sheet

Rolling pin

Cookie cutters

Small sieve or garlic press

Toothpicks

Decorative slotted spoon

Watercolors or poster paints

Paint brushes

Varnish (spray or can)

Krazy Glue

Christmas-ornament hangers

In a large bowl, stir together the flour, salt, and ¾ cup water until well combined. The dough will feel stiff and slightly dry. Knead the dough for several minutes—if crumbly, add water; if the dough becomes sticky, add more flour. (For children, the dough should be drier since it becomes soft in their hands.) Wrap the dough in plastic wrap and let it rest 1 hour (do not refrigerate).

Make the ornaments as described below or as desired. If you want a hole in the ornament for hanging, pierce a hole in the dough with a wooden toothpick before baking. To dry out the ornaments, bake in a 250° F. oven for 1 to 2 hours, depending on thickness. Alternately, ornaments can be air-dried, though this will take several days or weeks depending on their size, the thickness of the ornaments, and the humidity of the room.

Paint the ornaments as desired. When the paint is completely dry, coat the ornament with varnish. Two coats of thick varnish will give the ornament a high gloss and protect it against humidity and damage.

Attach hangers to the ornaments with glue or through a hole poked in the ornament.

DESIGNS

Candle: One of the easiest ornaments for little craftsmen. Simply roll a piece of dough about 4½ inches long and ½ inch wide. Trim the bottom end straight; trim the top of the candle at a diagonal. Place on a cookie sheet and straighten the sides with a ruler if necessary. Make a flame by rolling a small piece of dough into a ball; taper one end and attach it to the top of candlestick. (When baked, the flame will stick to the candle, but it should be reinforced with glue before hanging.)

continued

Letters: Roll strips of dough and shape them into letters as desired. Any size can be made, though larger letters can be pierced at the top to make a hole for the ornament hanger.

Candy Cane: Roll two strips of dough about ½ inch wide and 6 inches long. Cross one strip over the other at the center to make an X; twist both ends to make the candy cane. With a toothpick or skewer, poke a small hole at the top of the cane to hang it as an ornament.

Cookie-Cutter Ornaments: Dinosaur, rocking horse, "peace" hand. With a rolling pin, roll out the dough to a thickness of ¼ to ½ inch on a work surface or right on an ungreased cookie sheet. Press the cookie cutters, spaced closely together, into the dough. Remove the dough trimmings and reuse.

For a rocking horse, add the horse's mane by pressing the dough through a garlic press to make thin strands of dough. Poke a small hole at the top of the horse to hang it as an ornament.

For a "peace" hand, carefully move the fingers of the dough hand into place; make markings of nails on the pinky and thumb. (Glue an ornament hanger on the back of the hand after drying, painting, and varnishing.)

Teddy Bear: Make one round of dough about 2 inches in diameter for the bear's belly; place on a cookie sheet. Make a smaller round of dough for the bear's head; attach to the larger round. Make four small rounds of dough and attach as legs and arms.

Pinch two tiny rounds of dough to make ears; attach to the head. Make a tiny round of dough for the nose and attach to the center of the head. (Glue an ornament hanger on the back of the bear after drying, painting, and varnishing.) Teddy Bear will take longer than most to dry out because his body is thick.

Decorative Medallion: Make by pressing a smooth, thick, oval piece of dough into a decoratively slotted spoon, so some of the dough is forced through the holes of the spoon. Carefully pull the dough out of the spoon, being careful not to damage the design of the spoon on the dough. Poke a small hole at the top of the medallion to hang it as an ornament.

Santa Claus: Shape a piece of dough into an oval about the size of a large soup spoon; place on a cookie sheet. To make Santa's cap, shape another piece of dough into a thick triangle; pull the top of the triangle so it curves slightly downward as a stocking cap would. Attach a small ball of dough at the end of the stocking cap. Make Santa's eyes and cheeks using tiny rounds of dough; create the nose and mouth using tiny rolled strips of dough, curved in a circle for the mouth, straight for the nose. To make Santa's beard, mustache, and eyebrows, press the dough through a garlic press or small sieve to create strands of dough; attach to the face. Pinch tiny balls of dough for the ears and attach. Poke a small hole in Santa's cap to hang it as an ornament.

✄ *Makes about 3 pounds of dough, enough for about 15 3-inch ornaments*

Part II

THE GIFT OF HOSPITALITY

The gift of hospitality is an acquired art. It involves two skills. One is easy and the other is more difficult. The easy part is to do a lot of careful planning well in advance. Tackle a dinner party for two or twenty with as much care as you devote to any professional enterprise. Think it through carefully, making sure the menu is made up of dishes that you know you can make without worrying about them. They should not be be too complicated or time-consuming, nor stretch the budget to the point of anxiety.

Consider where everyone is to sit. Decide whether you have enough plates, cutlery, and serving dishes. Make a shopping list and a timetable. Then abandon most of the decisions you have made.

And here we come to the difficult part. Be flexible. Don't despair if you suddenly find you have to make last-minute changes. As long as you are happy, everyone else will be, too.

Share the work if you can. Put a friend in charge of the music, ask others to set the table, buy the wine, bring the food to the table after you have cooked it, and take it away again at the end of each course. There should be a plan for the clearing up, but we won't worry about that here. It will get done. Eventually.

I am very keen on the whole idea of excess. I love having big baskets of bread to pass, large pots of butter, and plenty of everything. Though I know it won't all be eaten, I don't worry. It will be there for another day. I like big wineglasses and I like having the bottle on the table where I can reach it without waiting for someone else to feel responsible about noticing that I would like some more, please.

I am inordinately fond of cheese and like having a cheese course at my parties. It is anachronistic, of course, and at first almost everyone declines to have any. Yet, oddly, there is rarely much left when it comes time to take away the plates.

One of the best cheeses to have at Christmastime is Stilton, with a few walnuts, shelled at table, and a ripe pear and a drop or two of port. This small snack can be offered anytime after 11:00 A.M. as an alternative to a toasted muffin and a cup of tea. Some people really do prefer the tea. Hospitable people know just what is good for others to try and what will please them most. It is not entirely inhospitable, though, to please yourself as long as you offer to share your treasure.

It is essential to have the very best of everything on hand during the Christmas season. There is no knowing what Santa may ask for, and as he will have little time, it is wise to be prepared for any request. Therefore, may I suggest that you add to your shopping list, in addition to everything you have already thought of, all those other things that you would like for yourself.

And don't forget the licorice. Someone is sure to ask if you have any.

A Colander of Fresh Crudités with Creamy Salsa Dip

Mulled Wine

French Onion Soup Bourgignon with Gruyère Croutons
Baked Ziti with Creamy Vegetables
Roast Duck Salad with Fennel, Oranges, and Rosemary

Chocolate Wreath Cake

Chapter Six

A Tree-Trimming Party for Twelve (or More)

We have a tradition in our family that began when we lived in a small village. We had been invited to a neighbor's house for a simple glass of wine and arrived a little early with the children and the dogs. We rang the doorbell and in the few minutes before it was answered, we began to sing "Good King Wenceslas." Our host threw the door open and in a fraction of a moment his whole family came running to see what was happening. Amid a lot of laughter everyone joined in the singing. "Let's go and sing some more carols," said a voice. And we did.

And before long there was a group of twenty and then thirty of us and all the dogs frolicking along, happily going from door to door, singing (mostly off-key) and forgetting the words and filling in with a lot of fa-la-las, and then we all came back to our house where we drank new Beaujolais, which was all the rage at that time, and I finished off some onion soup that I had started earlier in the day.

And with many willing hands to help, we threw together a huge bowl of pasta, because it was easy and quick to make, and added masses of colorful vegetables and warm olive oil and a handful of cheese and we had an instant dinner. Simple, good, and easy—and ready in barely half an hour. (I offer a baked version, enriched with a splash of cream.) The candles were lit and some sat at the table and some on the couch and others draped themselves around the fire, and a ravishing, just-home-from-college-within-the-hour young couple played their guitars and sang their own sweet songs. It was a night carved in memory. It was Christmas as Christmas should always be.

We left the neighborhood a few years later, but the tradition continues. In memory of that happy night we still sing carols on Christmas Eve and invite a few friends to come and join us and help us decorate our Christmas tree . . . and stay for supper.

There are always plenty of morsels to nibble on, and then an expandable feast in case several surprise guests come at the last minute. Everyone is always welcome.

It is a relaxed, informal evening, and to decorate the table I often arrange a collection of fresh vegetables in a colander. The guests usually eat everything, including the centerpiece.

A Colander of Fresh Crudités with Creamy Salsa Dip

Nothing could be easier than this zippy dip that is excelente *with tortilla chips as well as crudités.*

1½ cups salsa, homemade or store-bought
1 cup sour cream
2 scallions, finely chopped
¼ cup chopped fresh coriander (cilantro), optional
Assorted crudités, such as carrots, celery sticks, jicama sticks, cherry tomatoes, broccoli and cauliflower florets

In a medium bowl, stir together the salsa, sour cream, scallions, and coriander. (The dip can be prepared up to 1 day ahead, covered and refrigerated. Stir well before serving.)

In a colander, arrange the crudités and serve with the dip.

Mulled Wine

Once a year, I love to have mulled wine. It is like holding hands from generation to generation. I make mine in a beautiful old copper stockpot and keep it warm over the lowest possible flame. It fills the kitchen and house with the scent of Christmas.

2 750-ml bottles decent, but not great or expensive, red wine
2 cups water
⅓ cup honey
1 teaspoon Angostura bitters
1 teaspoon whole allspice berries
1 teaspoon ground nutmeg
12 cloves
2 cinnamon sticks
Zest of 1 orange, removed with a vegetable peeler

Pour the wine, water, honey, and bitters into a large saucepan. Wrap the allspice, nutmeg, cloves, cinnamon sticks, and orange zest in a square of cheesecloth and tie with string. Add the spice bag to the pan and heat the wine, uncovered, over very low heat until hot, about 30 minutes. Place the saucepan on a flame-tamer, so the wine never boils. Remove the spice bag and serve the mulled wine hot.

Serves 12 to 16

French Onion Soup Bourgignon with Gruyère Croutons

Onion soup is always wildly popular thanks to its romantic associations with French cafés and memories of happy times. Here's a recipe that is easy to serve, ladled into coffee cups and floated with a cheese-coated crouton.

8 tablespoons (1 stick) unsalted butter

8 large yellow onions, thinly sliced (about 4 pounds)

2 teaspoons sugar

¼ cup all-purpose flour

6 cups chicken stock or canned low-sodium broth

2 cups red wine

1 teaspoon salt

2 teaspoons dried thyme

¼ teaspoon freshly ground black pepper

12 ½-inch-thick French baguette slices

2 tablespoons olive oil

½ cup grated Gruyère cheese

Heat the butter in a large soup kettle and add the onions. Cover, and cook over medium heat, stirring often, for 20 to 30 minutes, until the onions have wilted. Transfer the onions to a large skillet and sprinkle with the sugar. Cook, uncovered, over medium-high heat, stirring often, until the onions are a rich brown color, about 25 minutes. Stir in the flour and cook for 1 minute. Using a wire whisk, stir in 2 cups of the chicken broth gradually to prevent the flour from forming lumps. Return the onion mixture to the kettle. Stir in the remaining chicken broth and the wine. Add the salt and thyme. Simmer, uncovered, over low heat for 40 minutes, until the soup has reduced slightly. Season with pepper.

In the meantime, preheat the oven to 400° F. Put the slices of bread on a baking sheet, brush with the oil, and bake 10 to 15 minutes, until toasted. Remove from the oven and sprinkle with the cheese. Return to the oven and bake until the cheese is melted, about 5 minutes.

Ladle the soup into coffee cups or paper cups with handles. Float a piece of cheese crouton in each cup.
✖ *Serves 12*

French Onion Soup Bourgignon with Gruyère Croutons, Roast Duck Salad with Fennel, Oranges, and Rosemary

Baked Ziti with Creamy Vegetables

A colorful, carefree entrée that everyone in the family will love—including the cook who can prepare it ahead of time! Since many of my guests have announced their intentions to increase their vegetable and grain intake, I think it is a thoughtful host or hostess who offers vegetarian fare at these large gatherings. Make your own from-scratch vegetable stock, or use the vegetable bouillon cubes found at health-food stores and many supermarkets. (Chicken broth works just fine, too.) Other vegetables can be added at will—artichoke hearts, fennel, celery, mushrooms—but try this Provençale-inspired mélange.

1 head broccoli, stems pared and chopped, and the remainder cut into small florets
2 pounds large tubular pasta, such as ziti or mostaccioli
6 tablespoons olive oil
2 medium red onions, sliced
1 medium sweet red pepper, seeded and chopped
1 medium sweet yellow pepper, seeded and chopped
4 garlic cloves, minced
2 medium zucchini, quartered lengthwise and cut into ½-inch-thick pieces
2 medium yellow squash, quartered lengthwise and cut into ½-inch-thick pieces
½ teaspoon salt
½ teaspoon freshly ground black pepper
2 cups heavy cream
2 cups vegetable stock or chicken broth, homemade or canned
1 cup grated imported Parmesan cheese
½ cup chopped fresh basil (optional)

In a large soup kettle of boiling lightly salted water, cook the chopped broccoli stems for 2 minutes. Add the florets and continue cooking until the broccoli is crisp-tender, about an additional 2 minutes. Using a slotted skimmer, transfer the broccoli to a colander. Rinse under cold water, drain well, and place in a very large bowl.

In the same kettle, add the pasta and cook, stirring often, until just tender, 6 to 8 minutes. Drain well, rinse under cold water, and toss with 1 tablespoon of the oil to avoid sticking. Add to the bowl with the broccoli.

In a large skillet, heat 3 tablespoons of the remaining oil over medium heat. Add the onions, red and yellow peppers, and garlic and cook, stirring often, until the onions are softened, about 8 minutes. Transfer the vegetables to the bowl.

In the same skillet, heat the remaining 2 tablespoons of oil. Add the zucchini and yellow squash and cook over medium-high heat, stirring often, until crisp-tender, about 5 minutes. Transfer to the bowl, season with the salt and pepper, and stir well.

Lightly oil two large baking dishes. (Lasagne-sized dishes, about 9 by 13 inches, are fine, but I use two round glazed clay "paella pans," about 12 inches wide and 3 inches deep.) Divide the pasta mixture evenly between the prepared dishes. (The dishes can be prepared up to 6 hours ahead, cooled, covered with plastic wrap, and set aside at cool room temperature.)

Preheat the oven to 400° F. In a large measuring cup, mix the heavy cream and broth. Pour 2 cups of the liquid into each dish. Sprinkle each dish with ½ cup Parmesan cheese. Bake until the cheese is melted and the pasta is lightly browned, about 30 minutes. Let the pasta stand for 5 minutes, then sprinkle with the basil, if desired, and serve directly from the baking dishes.

✄ *Makes 12 servings*

Roast Duck Salad with Fennel, Oranges, and Rosemary

I adore this salad. When guests are invited for lunch I often spend ages trying to decide what to make—and at least half the time, this is the thing I choose. If you live near a Chinese community, buy two ready-roasted ducks from an Oriental delicatessen.

2 4- to 5-pound ducks, seasoned with salt and
     pepper, roasted on a rack in a preheated
     350° F. oven for 2 hours and cooled
1 head fennel, finely chopped
6 stalks celery, finely chopped
1 medium red onion, finely chopped
8 navel oranges

THE DRESSING
¼ cup white-wine vinegar
¾ cup olive oil
Grated zest of 2 oranges
½ teaspoon Dijon mustard
2 teaspoons dried rosemary, crumbled
1 teaspoon salt
¼ teaspoon freshly ground black pepper

2 bunches watercress
1 cup chopped toasted walnuts, for garnish

Remove all the meat from the ducks, discarding the skin and any fat. Cut the meat into bite-sized pieces. (Save the bones—they will be a delicious addition to the Christmas stock pot.) Combine the duck, fennel, celery, and red onion in a bowl. Cut off the peel and pith from all the oranges. Cut them into ½-inch-thick rounds, and set aside. The duck mixture can be prepared up to 1 day ahead, covered and refrigerated.

To make the dressing: Place the ingredients in a jar with a tight-fitting lid and shake vigorously until thoroughly combined.

Moisten the duck mixture with the dressing. Line a serving platter with watercress and mound the duck salad in the center. Garnish with orange rounds and chopped walnuts.

✗ *Serves 12*

Chocolate Wreath Cake

This lovely wreath cake is deceivingly simple to make. It's an old-fashioned two-step: Just add the wets to the dries. The result is a moist, rich, dark chocolate cake. It is elegantly decorated with a poured butter icing and a few sprigs of buttercream holly.

3 cups all-purpose flour
1 tablespoon baking powder
1 tablespoon baking soda
1½ cup teaspoons salt
3 cups sugar
3 cups water
6 ounces semisweet chocolate, finely chopped
1 pound (4 sticks) unsalted butter, softened
3 large eggs, lightly beaten
2¼ cups confectioners' sugar
½ teaspoon vanilla extract
Few drops green food coloring
Fresh raspberries, dried cranberries, or cherries,
    for garnish

Preheat the oven to 350° F. Butter and flour a 10-inch tube pan with a nonremovable bottom.

In a large bowl, sift together the flour, baking powder, baking soda, and salt. In a medium pot, combine the sugar and water and bring them to the boil. Remove the pot from the heat and stir in the chocolate and 1 stick of butter. When the chocolate and butter have completely melted, whisk the mixture to combine completely. Whisk in the beaten eggs. Pour about half the chocolate mixture into the dry ingredients and whisk vigorously to thoroughly combine the ingredients and remove any lumps. Working quickly, add the remaining chocolate mixture and whisk to combine. Pour the batter into the prepared pan and bake for about 60 minutes, until a cake tester inserted in the center comes out clean. Let the cake cool in the pan for about 15 minutes, then turn out onto a rack to cool completely.

In a medium bowl, cream together the remaining 3 sticks of butter and the confectioners' sugar, until light and fluffy. Remove ⅓ cup of the icing, place in a small bowl, and color it with a few drops of the green food coloring. Put the remaining icing in a pot, add the vanilla. Over low heat, stir the icing until it becomes a pourable consistency. (If it overheats, causing the butter to separate, put the icing in the refrigerator to chill and stir to bring it back together.) Pour the icing over the cooled cake so that it drips down the center and outside. Cluster the red berries in groups of 3 on top of the cake. Fill the green icing into a pastry bag fitted with a leaf tip and pipe a few leaves around each cluster of berries.

✻ *Serves 12 to 16*

Swiss Cheese Fondue with Crudités, New Potatoes, and
Cornichons
Two-Meat, Two-Bean Chili
Marinated Salmon with Dill and Sweet Mustard Sauce
Broccoli Salad with Sweet Red Peppers

The Best Fruit Cake
Cakey Gingerbread Squares

New Wave Eggnog
Mulled Wine (see page 97)

Chapter Seven

An Open House for Twenty-five

An open house can be a horribly boring affair—a duty call. Everyone gets dressed up even though we don't want to. And there is much moaning and groaning because no one really wants to go, but we must. We barely arrive before we are getting ready to leave, responding in unison to our prearranged signals. We declare how happy we are to have come and dash through the door after a barely decent interval has elapsed.

The other kind of open house is easy and relaxed, one of those occasions that was supposed to last only three hours, but where we all linger on and on because we are having such a good time. Naturally, this sort of happy party is the one we stage ourselves. The menu has something for every appetite: mugs of chili for those who are famished and require a meal, or marinated salmon or fondue for those who have come to graze. The only "theme" the menu has is good, solid, easy-to-serve food.

The decorations are in keeping with the spirit of the party. When guests arrive in comfortable clothing and sneakers, the food, the table settings, and the decorations should hang together to harmonize with the atmosphere. Don't even think about buying a formal flower arrangement from the florist. Instead, fill a wooden bowl with crisp red and green apples or two dozen beautiful brown eggs. See what simple fresh flowers are available and slip colorful anemones or blue cornflowers among the eggs. Daisies look marvelous clumped in a faience teapot. Arrange clementines and walnuts in their shells and shiny green bay leaves in a colored bowl. (I have a cherished dark-blue willow-pattern dish that is just right for this kind of arrangement. It is very old and has a crack in it, but no one ever notices.)

Gather several different kinds of bread—long loaves, crusty country loaves, pumpernickel bread, croissants, brioches, and small rolls—and arrange them in a big basket. If you coat them with shellac, they will last for weeks. They will not be edible, though, so make sure people don't try to eat them.

There are so many simple things you can do to make

the table look attractive. Float a winter chrysanthemum or orchids in a tall wine glass. Along a table runner, arrange a long row of red, green, and yellow peppers, small eggplants, tomatoes, artichokes, persimmons, pears, and lemons. I like to use edible decorations on the table itself, even though they are not to be eaten at that precise moment.

Make the food sparkle. Use a dramatic tablecloth. (You could make one yourself out of silver lamé and scatter gleaming cutout stars and crescent moons over it.) Arrange the food in diagonal lines instead of the predictably straight ones. Elevate the dishes to different heights on cake stands or inverted bowls. (This gives the table drama and makes the food look wonderfully appealing.)

Pull the table away from the wall so that guests can serve themselves from both sides. Put the china and silver on another table so that the traffic will move quickly. Make sure there are plenty of glasses, but don't serve the wine already poured into them. Put several bottles of wine and mineral water close at hand. There is nothing worse than thirst at a party.

Have a good time!

Swiss Cheese Fondue with Crudités, New Potatoes, and Cornichons

Of all the thousands of meals eaten in one's lifetime, just a few stand apart and become crystallized in memory. One of my own happiest recollections is of sharing cheese fondue with a dear, dear friend in Gruyère, a tiny village in Switzerland. It was snowing. (In all my memories of Christmas it is snowing.) The tiny steamed potatoes, exquisite vegetables, cornichons, coarse salt, wonderful hot, freshly baked bread, and crisp white Dôle wine were all part of the fantasy enshrined in my remembrance.

1 clove garlic, peeled and halved
2 cups dry white wine
1 pound Gruyère cheese, grated
1 pound top-quality Swiss cheese (such as
    Emmentaler), grated
Freshly ground black pepper
2 tablespoons cornstarch dissolved in 2
    tablespoons kirsch
Crusty French bread cut into 1-inch cubes, for
    dipping

FOR SERVING
Fresh crudités, such as baby carrots, celery sticks,
    and endive spears
Small new potatoes, freshly boiled and still warm
Cornichons
Radishes

Rub the garlic all over the inside of an enameled cast-iron fondue pot. Discard the garlic. Add the wine. Place the pot over medium heat until the wine begins to simmer. Add the cheeses, a little at a time, stirring slowly with a wooden spoon in a figure-eight pattern. When all the cheese has melted, season with pepper to taste.

Stir the dissolved cornstarch into the cheese mixture. Continue stirring until the mixture has thickened, about 2 to 3 minutes. Place the fondue over a small burner at the table. Spear the bread on fondue forks or toothpicks and dip it into the cheese, which will gradually cook more and more and become crust-ier on the bottom.

Serve with small new potatoes, freshly boiled or steamed with their skins on, crisp French cornichons, and radishes. (Leave some of their green leaves on after you have scrubbed them; the tufts add a jaunty touch.)

Note: If you don't have a fondue pot or the correct long thin forks for dipping into the cheese, you can use a deep heavy saucepan set on a hot plate and conventional forks instead. A little of the charisma will be lost but the fondue will taste just as good.

✄ *Makes 25 appetizer servings*

Two-Meat, Two-Bean Chili

One of the best ways to serve a crowd (especially on a December evening) is a big batch of chili. This version uses both ground beef and hot Italian sausage for depth of flavor, and two kinds of beans for color. Making it well ahead allows the seasonings to mellow and the cook to relax at serving time. Put out bowls of sour cream, grated Cheddar cheese, sliced olives, chopped onions, and minced chile peppers for each guest to sprinkle on top of the chili.

5 pounds ground round (15 percent lean ground beef)

2 pounds hot or sweet Italian sausage, removed from casings, crumbled

3 large onions, chopped

2 medium sweet red bell peppers, seeded and chopped

2 medium green bell peppers, seeded and chopped

2 fresh hot green chile peppers, seeded and minced (or more to taste)

4 garlic cloves, minced

⅓ cup chili powder

1 tablespoon salt

2 teaspoons dried oregano

2 teaspoon ground cumin

2 bay leaves

3 28-ounce cans whole tomatoes with tomato puree, undrained

½ cup yellow cornmeal

2 16-ounce cans pink beans, drained

2 16-ounce cans black beans, drained

In a large soup kettle, cook the ground round, sausage, onions, red and green bell peppers, chile peppers, and garlic over medium-high heat, stirring often, until the meat is seared (but not browned), about 10 minutes. Pour off excess fat. Add the chili powder, salt, oregano, cumin, and bay leaves and stir for 1 minute. Add the tomatoes with their puree, breaking up the tomatoes with a spoon. Bring to a simmer. Reduce the heat to low and cook, stirring often, until the liquid is reduced, about 1½ hours.

In a small bowl, combine the cornmeal and ½ cup of water. Stir the cornmeal mixture and the pink and black beans into the chili. Cook, stirring occasionally, until the chili is thickened, about 10 minutes. (The chili can be made up to 3 days ahead. If desired, scrape off and discard the solidified fat that rises to the surface. Reheat the chili gently on top of the stove before serving.)

✖ *Makes about 25 servings*

Marinated Salmon with Dill and Sweet Mustard Sauce

This classic dish is known in its native land, Sweden, as graavlax. *It is one of my all-time favorites. Fresh dill is absolutely essential. Serve the salmon with pumpernickel bread slices, minced onion, capers, and lemon slices, so each guest can make mini-sandwiches.*

MARINATED SALMON

2 salmon fillets (1½ pounds each), preferably
  center cut
3 tablespoons kosher (coarse) salt
3 tablespoons sugar
1½ tablespoons black peppercorns, crushed
1 large bunch dill, rinsed, left whole

SWEET MUSTARD SAUCE

¼ cup Dijon mustard
3 tablespoons brown sugar
2 tablespoon white-wine vinegar
1 teaspoon powdered mustard
⅓ cup vegetable oil
3 tablespoons finely chopped fresh dill

To marinate the salmon: Using tweezers, pull out all the bones from the salmon fillets. (Feel along the sides of the fillets to locate the thin bones.) Combine the salt, sugar, and crushed peppercorns in a small bowl and mix well.

Place the salmon fillets skin side down on a work surface. Coat each salmon fillet evenly with the salt mixture. Place one of the fillets, skin side down, on a large piece of plastic wrap. Top with the dill, breaking the dill to fit the fillet, if necessary. Carefully place the second fillet, skin side up, on top of the dill. Tightly wrap the sandwiched fillets in the plastic, then over-wrap with aluminum foil.

Place the wrapped salmon in a shallow glass or enamel dish. Place a flat dish or board on top, and weight evenly with heavy cans of food. (The heavy weight and the salt will force the liquid out of the fish, leaving it firm and easy to slice.)

Put the salmon in the refrigerator and leave it to marinate for 3 or 4 days, turning it every other day. Remove the salmon from its wrapping and gently scrape off and discard the seasonings. Pat the fish dry with a paper towel.

To make the sweet mustard sauce: In a small bowl, whisk the Dijon mustard, brown sugar, vinegar, and powdered mustard until smooth. Gradually whisk in the oil. Stir in the dill. (The sweet mustard sauce can be made up to 3 days ahead, covered, and refrigerated.)

To serve, place the salmon, skin side down, on a wooden board. Slice it very thinly on the bias, using a sharp, thin-bladed knife, held almost horizontally. Lift the slices from the skin, and arrange on a serving platter. (The salmon can be sliced up to 6 hours ahead, covered tightly with aluminum foil, and refrigerated.) Serve the sliced salmon with the sweet mustard sauce.
✖ *Makes about 25 appetizer servings*

Broccoli Salad with Sweet Red Peppers

Leafy green salads easily wilt on a buffet table, but this tooth-some salad will hold up beautifully. Don't toss the vegetables with the dressing until the last minute, however, as the vinaigrette will alter the color of the broccoli after a few hours.

6 tablespoons rice-wine vinegar
2 teaspoons salt
¼ teaspoon freshly ground black pepper
¾ cup vegetable oil
¾ cup olive oil
2 large heads broccoli, stems pared and cut into
    ½-inch slices, and the remainder cut into
    florets
4 medium sweet red peppers, seeded and cut into
    ¾-inch pieces
8 scallions, finely chopped
¾ cup finely chopped fresh basil or parsley
1 cup Mediterranean black olives, pitted and
    coarsely chopped

In a medium bowl, whisk the vinegar, salt, and pepper. Gradually whisk in the vegetable and olive oils until smooth. (The dressing can be prepared up to 2 days ahead, covered, and refrigerated. Whisk well before using.)

In a large saucepan of lightly salted boiling water, cook the broccoli stems for 2 minutes. Add the broccoli florets and continue cooking until the broccoli is crisp-tender, about an additional 2 minutes. Drain, rinse under cold running water, and drain again. Pat the broccoli dry with paper towels. (The broccoli can be prepared up to 1 day ahead, wrapped in paper towels, stored in plastic bags, and refrigerated.)

In a large serving bowl, combine the broccoli, sweet peppers, scallions, basil, and olives. Add the dressing and toss well. Serve immediately.

✗ *Makes about 25 servings*

The Best Fruit Cake

Not one person will make a fruit-cake joke when they taste this one—the world's best! Glacé apricots and citrus rinds can be ordered from Williams-Sonoma, 1-800-541-2233.

2 cups golden raisins
2 cups dark raisins
2 cups glacé cherries, left whole
1 cup coarsely chopped candied pineapple rings
1¾ cups chopped glacé citrus rinds (use lemon or orange rinds, or both)
2 cups chopped Australian glacé apricots (about 1 pound)
1 cup sliced almonds
1 cup Brazil nuts or walnuts, very finely chopped
3 cups all-purpose flour, divided
1 teaspoon salt
2 teaspoons baking soda
1 teaspoon ground cinnamon
1 teaspoon ground allspice
½ teaspoon ground nutmeg
½ teaspoon ground cloves
1 cup (2 sticks) unsalted butter, softened
1½ cups packed dark-brown sugar
8 large eggs, lightly beaten
2 teaspoons vanilla extract
4 ounces semisweet chocolate, finely chopped
½ cup apple brandy, divided
Light corn syrup, for brushing
Candied whole fruits, crystallized ginger, and whole nuts, for garnish

Preheat the oven to 325° F. Butter and flour three 8- by 4- by 3-inch cake pans.

Toss all the fruits and nuts with 1 cup of the flour. (A dishwashing bowl is good for this.) Sift the remaining flour with the salt, baking soda, and spices.

Using a hand-held electric mixer set at high speed, beat the butter until creamy, about 1 minute. Add the sugar and beat until light in texture, about 2 minutes. At low speed, beat in the eggs in thirds alternately with the sifted flour mixture. Stir in the vanilla, chocolate, and apple brandy. Fold this mixture into the floured fruits and nuts. Transfer the cake mixture to the prepared pans and cover with oiled aluminum foil. Bake in the preheated oven for 1¼ hours, then remove the foil and continue cooking for an additional 20 minutes, or until a cake tester inserted into the center comes out clean.

Leave the cakes to cool in their pans for 15 minutes, then turn them out onto a wire rack and allow to cool completely. Wrap the cakes tightly in foil and store in the refrigerator for up to 1 month. To decorate, brush the cake's surface with corn syrup. Make an attractive pattern with additional crystallized fruits and nuts and tie a red ribbon around the sides.

✂ *Makes 3 8- by 4- by 3-inch cakes*

Cakey Gingerbread Squares

Christmastime is gingerbread season! Gingerbread cookies, gingerbread houses, and this comforting gingerbread cake are just three examples of the genre. This cake is at its best served warm with whipped cream or vanilla ice cream. For twenty-five guests, you will want to double, or even triple, this recipe. It is best to make and bake them one at a time.

8 tablespoons (1 stick) unsalted butter,
    at room temperature
½ cup sugar
2 large eggs
Grated zest of 1 orange
2½ cups sifted all-purpose flour
2 teaspoons baking soda
2 teaspoons ground ginger
1 teaspoon ground cinnamon
½ teaspoon ground allspice
½ teaspoon ground nutmeg
½ teaspoon salt
¼ teaspoon ground cloves
1 cup unsulfured molasses
1 cup boiling water
Confectioners' sugar, for dusting

Preheat the oven to 350°F. Butter and flour a 9-inch-square baking pan.

Using a hand-held electric mixer set at high speed, beat the butter until creamy, about 1 minute. Add the sugar and beat until light in color and texture, about 2 additional minutes. Beat in the eggs and orange zest.

Sift the flour, baking soda, ginger, cinnamon, allspice, nutmeg, salt, and cloves onto a piece of waxed paper. In a 2-cup glass measuring cup, combine the molasses and boiling water. Alternately in thirds, beat in the flour and molasses mixtures. Transfer the batter to the prepared pan.

Bake until a toothpick inserted in the center of the cake comes out clean, and the cake is shrinking from the sides of the pan, 40 to 50 minutes. Let stand on a wire cake rack for 5 minutes.

Place the confectioners' sugar in a sieve and dust over the top of the cake. Serve the cake warm or completely cooled.

✖ *Makes 12 to 16 servings*

New Wave Eggnog

Many people are concerned about consuming foods that contain uncooked eggs. Some of our favorite dishes, such as hollandaise and eggnog, have suddenly become controversial. In order to allow my friends the pleasure of safely enjoying spirited holiday eggnog, I offer this version, where the mixture is cooked to a high-enough temperature to kill any unwanted bacteria. A "float" of vanilla ice cream helps keep the punch bowl of eggnog nicely chilled.

4 cups half-and-half
1½ cups sugar
12 large egg yolks
2 cups heavy cream
½ cup dark rum
½ cup brandy or cognac
½ cup bourbon or scotch
1 pint high-quality vanilla ice cream

In a medium saucepan, combine the half-and-half and sugar. Cook over low heat, stirring often, until the mixture comes to a low simmer. In a medium bowl, whisk the egg yolks until combined. Gradually whisk the hot mixture into the yolks. Return the yolk mixture to the saucepan. Cook over low heat, stirring constantly with a wooden spoon, until the custard lightly coats the spoon. (An instant-read thermometer inserted in the custard will read 180° F.) Immediately strain the custard through a sieve into a large bowl. Cool to room temperature, then cover with plastic wrap and refrigerate until very cold, at least 4 hours or overnight.

When ready to serve, whip the cream until soft peaks form. Stir the whipped cream, rum, brandy, and bourbon into the chilled custard. (The eggnog can be prepared up to 1 day ahead, covered, and refrigerated.)

Pour the eggnog into a punch bowl. Place the vanilla ice cream in the punch bowl and serve.

✖ *Makes about 1¾ quarts*

Parmesan Cheese and Rosemary Thins
Cheddar-Chive Popcorn
Herbed Mini Pizzas
Herbed Cheese Puffs
Fresh Crabmeat Salad in Endive Leaves
Goat Cheese Wontons with Red Pepper Dip
Smoked Salmon and Shrimp "Pâté" on Cucumber
Rounds
Wild Mushroom Caviar Tartlets
White Wine   Red Wine   Mineral Water

Chapter Eight

The Holiday Cocktail Party for Twenty-five

If you are like me, every holiday season you realize how many friends you'd meant to see more often during the year, but you just didn't get around to it. Invitations go out to these dear people to attend my annual holiday cocktail party, so with one sweep I can "clear the decks," socially speaking.

I love the excitement of a cocktail party—everyone looking smashing, delicious food, and stimulating talk. But cocktail food, so often made as individual servings and passed on trays, can be torture for a host or hostess. Don't spend all your time in the kitchen and not with your guests! I have given make-ahead instructions for all the hors d'oeuvres recipes in this chapter. Make them early and simply pop them into the oven to warm up before serving. Also, put out big bowls of dips and spreads so that guests can help themselves. From other chapters, Creamy Salsa Dip (page 97), Italian Eggplant and Tuna Spread (page 137), or Swiss Cheese Fondue (page 108) are just a few appropriate items to serve with toasted baguette slices, crackers, chips, or crudités.

Probably the best advice I can offer is to hire someone to come in and help out, warming up and passing the hors d'oeuvres, picking up and washing glasses, and hanging up coats. Call a maid service or the local college employment office and see what they can offer. If you keep your beverages simple, you will not need a bartender. It is chic these days to simply offer red and white wines and sparkling mineral water, but at the holidays I will also add either Mulled Wine (page 97) or New Wave Eggnog (page 119) to my beverage menu.

Parmesan Cheese and Rosemary Thins

These crisp wafers are good to have on hand for nibbling with drinks. You can double the quantity for a crowd. In the unlikely event that there are any left over, they can be reheated for 5 minutes and served with a bowl of soup or a salad.

8 tablespoons (1 stick) unsalted butter, softened
1 tablespoon granulated sugar
1 large egg, beaten
½ teaspoon salt
¼ teaspoon coarsely ground black pepper
1 cup sifted all-purpose flour
¼ cup grated Parmesan cheese
4 teaspoons dried rosemary, divided

Using an electric mixer set at high speed, beat the butter and sugar in a large bowl until creamy, about 1 minute. Add the egg, salt, and pepper. Continue beating until just mixed. Stir in the flour, cheese and 2 teaspoons of the rosemary. Mix to form a soft dough. Wrap in waxed paper, form into a 10-inch-long cylinder, and chill for 1 hour.

Preheat the oven to 400° F.

Using a sharp, thin-bladed knife, slice ¼-inch-thick rounds of the chilled dough. Arrange the rounds on ungreased baking sheets, leaving about 1 inch between them. With a fork dipped in cold water, flatten the rounds of dough until they are very thin and about 2 inches in diameter. Sprinkle the flattened tops with the remaining rosemary and bake in the preheated oven for 6 to 8 minutes, or until the edges are golden. Remove from the oven, leave on the sheet to cool for 5 minutes, then use a metal spatula to transfer the wafers to a wire rack to cool completely. Repeat the process until all the dough has been baked.

The wafers can be made up to 3 days ahead, and stored in an airtight container.

✖ *Makes about 40*

Left to right: Smoked Salmon "Pâté" on Cucumber Rounds, Herbed Cheese Puffs, Parmesan Cheese and Rosemary Thins, Fresh Crabmeat Salad in Endive and Radicchio Leaves

Cheddar-Chive Popcorn

If the giant food companies could only duplicate this recipe they would surely make a fortune. It tastes much better than any packaged popcorn.

The cheese should be as dry as possible when added to the popcorn. Spread the grated cheese on a plate and chill it, uncovered, in the refrigerator, for several hours or overnight.

1 cup popcorn, popped (about 12 cups)
3 tablespoons unsalted butter, cut into small pieces
2 teaspoons white-wine Worcestershire sauce
3 cloves garlic, finely chopped
3 tablespoons dried chives
½ cup finely grated sharp Cheddar cheese, dried
    (see above)
Salt, to taste

Preheat the oven to 350° F.

Place the popcorn in a large bowl. Put the butter, Worcestershire sauce, and garlic in a small saucepan and cook over low heat for about 3 minutes until the garlic has softened. Add the chives and stir well. Pour over the popcorn and toss.

Spread the popcorn evenly in a large jelly-roll pan. Bake in the preheated oven for 15 minutes, removing the pan and stirring occasionally. Remove the pan from the oven. Toss the cheese with the popcorn, allow to cool slightly, then serve at once, adding salt to taste.
✗ *Makes 12 cups*

Herbed Mini Pizzas

Honor your guests with homemade pizza and they will sing your praises (and help you wash the dishes, too, if you are lucky).

THE DOUGH

1 package active dry yeast (a scant 2½ teaspoons)
Pinch of sugar
1 cup lukewarm water (100° to 110° F., but use
    cool water if making in a food processor)
1 tablespoon olive oil
3½ cups unbleached all-purpose flour
1 teaspoon salt

TOPPING

1 tablespoon fresh marjoram leaves, or 1 teaspoon
    dried
1 tablespoon fresh oregano leaves, or 1 teaspoon
    dried
1 tablespoon chopped fresh Italian parsley
1½ teaspoons olive oil
12 ounces soft goat cheese (chèvre)
2 tablespoons milk
¼ teaspoon salt
¼ teaspoon freshly ground black pepper

Cornmeal, for dusting
¼ cup black Mediterranean olives, pitted and
    halved
Strips of bottled roasted red pepper

To make the dough: Stir the yeast and the pinch of sugar into the lukewarm water and set aside until frothy, about 10 minutes. Stir to dissolve the yeast. Add the oil.

Put 3 cups of the flour and the salt in a large bowl.

Pour in the yeast mixture and mix to form a dough. Turn out onto a work surface and knead for 10 minutes, adding the remaining ½ cup of flour a little at a time, to achieve a smooth and elastic dough. (Or, place the flour and salt in a food processor fitted with the metal blade, and pulse to combine. With the machine running, add the yeast mixture and process to form a ball. [You may have to add a little more water.] Process for 45 seconds to knead.)

Place the dough in a clean, oiled bowl, turning the dough to coat lightly. Cover with plastic wrap and allow to rise for 1 hour, or until doubled in volume. Punch down the dough and allow to stand for 10 minutes.

To make the topping: Place the herbs, oil, goat cheese, milk, salt, and pepper in a food processor. Blend until smooth.

Preheat the oven to 475° F. Brush 2 baking sheets with a little olive oil and dust lightly with cornmeal.

Cut the dough into 8 equal pieces. Shape each piece of dough into a 6-inch-long log, then cut each log into 8 equal pieces, to give you 64 pieces in total. Pat each piece of dough into a 1½- to 2-inch round and place on the baking sheets, 1 inch apart.

Place 1 teaspoon of the cheese-and-herb topping on top of each pizza. Arrange an olive half and a strip of red pepper on top of each one. Bake in the preheated oven for 6 to 8 minutes, or until the dough is golden and the topping fragrant. Remove from the oven, transfer to a serving platter, and serve at once. Continue to make up and bake more trays of pizza until all the pieces have been cooked. (The mini-pizzas can be prepared up to 6 hours ahead, covered with plastic wrap, and stored at room temperature. Reheat the pizzas, as needed, for 5 to 10 minutes in a preheated 400° F. oven.)

✄ *Makes 64 pieces*

Herbed Cheese Puffs

The French call these cheese-and-tarragon-flavored morsels gougères. They are quick to make and can be reheated easily.

1 cup water
6 tablespoons (¾ stick) unsalted butter, cut up
½ teaspoon salt
1 cup all-purpose flour
2 teaspoons Dijon mustard
4 large eggs, at room temperature
½ cup finely grated Gruyère or Emmentaler cheese
½ cup grated imported Parmesan cheese
1 tablespoon chopped fresh tarragon leaves, or 1 teaspoon dried
1 large egg yolk
1 tablespoon milk

Heat the oven to 375° F. In a medium saucepan, bring the water, butter, and salt just to a full boil over medium heat. (Be sure the butter is melted.) Reduce the heat to low. Add the flour and stir vigorously until the dough forms a ball and a thin film forms on the bottom of the saucepan, about 1 minute. Remove from heat and cool for 1 minute. Beat in the mustard.

One at a time, add the eggs, beating well after each addition. Beat in the cheeses and tarragon. Transfer the dough to a pastry bag fitted with a large plain round decorating tip, such as Ateco Number 5. On ungreased baking sheets, pipe out the dough into 1-inch balls, spaced 1 inch apart. Beat the egg yolk with the milk and brush the tops of the balls with some of the yolk mixture.

Bake until the balls are puffed and firm, about 25 minutes. Quickly pierce the puffs with the tip of a sharp knife. (If the puffs collapse, return them to the oven for a few more minutes.) Return the puffs to the oven until crisp, about 5 additional minutes. Serve the puffs warm or at room temperature. (The puffs can be prepared up to 1 day ahead, covered, and stored at room temperature. Reheat the puffs in a 350° F. oven for 5 to 8 minutes.)

✖ *Makes about 6 dozen puffs*

Fresh Crabmeat Salad in Endive Leaves

Pale Belgian endive, dramatic red endive, or tiny Bibb lettuce leaves are all excellent edible containers for this spicy salad. Arrange the leaves on a brightly colored plate for a striking presentation.

⅓ cup prepared mayonnaise
¼ cup sour cream
1 tablespoon fresh lemon juice
1 teaspoon prepared horseradish
1 teaspoon Old Bay Seasoning
1 pound lump crabmeat, picked over for cartilage and flaked
2 celery ribs, finely chopped
1 small red bell pepper, seeded and finely chopped
2 scallions, finely chopped
3 to 4 heads baby Bibb lettuce or Belgian or red endive, separated into leaves

In a medium bowl, stir the mayonnaise, sour cream, lemon juice, horseradish, and Old Bay Seasoning until combined. Add the crabmeat, celery, red bell pepper, and scallion and mix. (The salad can be prepared up to 1 day ahead, covered tightly, and refrigerated.)

To serve, spoon about 1 tablespoon of the salad into the end of each leaf. (The leaves can be prepared up to 2 hours ahead, placed in rows on baking sheets and covered with plastic wrap. Refrigerate until ready to serve.) Serve chilled.

✕ *Makes about 50 appetizers*

Goat Cheese Wontons with Red Pepper Dip

This idea is inspired by the party menu at The Rainbow Room in New York City. It is sensational, especially because it seems so wicked to eat fried food!

THE FILLING

¼ cup pine nuts

2 tablespoons olive oil

1 bunch scallions, trimmed and finely chopped

2 cloves garlic, finely chopped

3 tablespoons chopped fresh coriander (cilantro) or basil

⅛ teaspoon salt

¼ teaspoon coarsely ground black pepper

3 tablespoons dry vermouth

10-ounce package frozen spinach, thawed and squeezed dry

6 ounces soft goat cheese (chèvre), crumbled

RED PEPPER SAUCE

2 7-ounce jars roasted red peppers, drained and coarsely chopped

1 bunch scallions, trimmed and finely chopped

1 clove garlic, finely chopped

¼ cup chicken stock or canned low-sodium broth

⅛ teaspoon salt

⅛ teaspoon freshly ground black pepper

1 package wonton wrappers
Vegetable oil for deep-frying

To make the filling: In a large, dry skillet, over medium-high heat, cook the pine nuts, stirring often, until lightly browned, about 2 minutes. Set aside on a plate. Heat the olive oil in the skillet over medium heat. Add the scallions and garlic and cook, stirring occasionally, until wilted, about 3 minutes. Add the coriander, salt, pepper, vermouth, and spinach and cook for 2 minutes, stirring constantly until the excess moisture is evaporated. Remove from the heat and stir in the goat cheese and pine nuts. Set aside to cool completely.

To make the red pepper sauce: Put the peppers, scallions, garlic, and chicken broth into a medium-sized saucepan and cook, uncovered, over medium heat for 15 minutes, stirring occasionally. Remove from the heat and allow to cool slightly. Transfer to a blender or food processor and blend until smooth. Season with the salt and pepper. Cool completely. (The sauce can be prepared up to 1 day ahead, covered, and refrigerated.)

To make the wontons: Working as quickly as possible to prevent the wrappers from drying out, arrange the wrappers on a work surface with a point facing toward you. Put 1 heaped teaspoon of filling just below the center of each wrapper. Brush the edges lightly with water. Bring the lower point of the wrapper up to cover the filling and almost meet at the opposite point. Fold the 2 side points in so that they almost meet at the top point. Using a drop of water to help the wrapper adhere, press to seal.

Pour oil for deep-frying into a deep-fryer or large skillet and heat until the oil reaches 365° F. (An electric skillet works well.) Fry the wontons in small batches for 1 to 2 minutes, turning once, until golden. Remove with a slotted spoon and lay them to drain on a baking sheet lined with several thicknesses of paper towels. Continue cooking the remaining wontons and draining them in the same way. (The wontons can be prepared up to 8 hours ahead, cooled completely, covered with plastic wrap, and refrigerated for up to 6 hours before serving.)

To serve, Uncover the wontons and reheat them in a preheated 400° F. oven for 10 minutes, or until just heated through. Warm the sauce gently over low heat, stirring occasionally, and serve with the wontons.

✖ *Makes about 36 wontons*

Smoked Salmon and Shrimp "Pâté" on Cucumber Rounds

Smoked salmon and cooked shrimp combine to make a seafood pâté that is dolloped onto crisp cucumber slices for a delicious hors d'oeuvre with an admirably low calorie count.

12 ounces smoked salmon, coarsely chopped
12 ounces cooked peeled shrimp, coarsely chopped
3 tablespoons finely chopped fresh dill
1 small yellow onion, finely chopped
3 tablespoons mayonnaise
1 teaspoon Dijon mustard
⅛ teaspoon freshly ground black pepper
2 long thin seedless English cucumbers, washed but not peeled, sliced into ¼-inch-thick rounds
Red or black caviar and sprigs of fresh dill, for garnish

Combine the smoked salmon, shrimp, dill, onion, mayonnaise, mustard, and pepper in a food processor

fitted with the metal blade and pulse until well combined and almost smooth. (The pâté can be made up to 1 day ahead, covered, and refrigerated.)

Place teaspoonfuls of the salmon mixture on top of each cucumber round. Garnish each one with morsels of caviar and/or tiny sprigs of dill. Serve at once.

✖ *Makes about 60 rounds*

Wild Mushroom Caviar Tartlets

Minced wild mushrooms cook down to a dark, full-flavored mixture that is served in tiny cream cheese pastry tartlets. Make both components the day before, and simply heat the filling up before spooning into the crusts. (Yes, you can use cultivated mushrooms and store-bought pastry shells, if you wish.)

CREAM CHEESE PASTRY

1 cup all-purpose flour

¼ teaspoon salt

8 tablespoons (1 stick) unsalted butter, chilled, cut into 1-inch pieces

1 3-ounce package cream cheese, cut into 1-inch pieces

WILD MUSHROOM CAVIAR

3 tablespoons olive oil

1 small onion, finely chopped

1 pound wild mushrooms, such as cremini, portobello, or stemmed shiitake, finely chopped (a food processor does the best job)

1 garlic clove, minced

4 tablespoons dry vermouth or white wine

2 teaspoons chopped fresh tarragon or ½ teaspoon dried tarragon

¼ teaspoon salt

⅛ teaspoon freshly ground black pepper

⅓ cup heavy cream

Sour cream and tarragon leaves, for garnish

To make the cream cheese tartlets: Preheat the oven to 375° F. In a food processor fitted with the metal blade, pulse the flour and salt to mix. Add the butter and cream cheese and pulse until crumbly. The mixture will not form a ball, but will hold together when pinched. Gather up into a ball, wrap in plastic wrap, and refrigerate for 30 minutes.

Using a heaping teaspoon of dough for each tartlet, press the dough firmly and evenly into 42 ungreased mini-muffin shells (1¾ inches wide and 1 inch deep). Prick the dough well with a fork. Bake until the crusts are lightly browned, about 10 minutes. Using a small sharp knife, lift out the crusts and cool completely on a wire rack. (The tartlet crusts can be made a day ahead and stored in an airtight container at room temperature.)

To make the filling: In a large skillet, heat the oil over medium heat. Add the onion and cook, stirring often, until softened, about 3 minutes. Add the mushrooms, garlic, dry vermouth, tarragon, salt, and pepper. Cover and cook until the mushrooms have given off their liquid, about 3 minutes. Uncover, increase the heat to medium-high, and cook, stirring often, until all the liquid has evaporated, about 10 minutes. Add the heavy cream and cook, stirring, until thickened, about 2 minutes. (The filling can be made up to 1 day ahead, cooled, covered, and refrigerated.)

To serve, reheat the mushroom mixture and spoon it into the tartlets. Garnish the top of each tartlet with a dab of sour cream (if desired, apply with a pastry bag fitted with a small open-star decorating tip, such as Ateco Number 2) and a tarragon leaf.

✖ *Makes about 40 tartlets*

Herbed Mini Pizzas, Wild Mushroom Caviar Tartlets

Italian Eggplant and Tuna Spread

Shrimp and Scallop Lasagne with Two Sauces

Green, White, and Red Salad with
Sundried-Tomato Pesto Dressing

Prosciutto and Parmesan Muffins

Amaretto Cheesecake

Pinot Grigio   Espresso   Sambuca

Chapter Nine

An Italian Seafood Christmas Eve Supper for Fourteen

Many of the best-known American Christmas foods reflect British traditions (probably thanks more to Charles Dickens than to any British chef). The flaming plum pudding, the rich-flavored fruit cake, the holiday toast of mulled wine or eggnog—all these were a part of my English holiday season.

But of course, each country has its own Yuletide menu, and Italy's Christmas Eve bill of fare is particularly mouthwatering. Each dish, appetizer, main dish, and side dish must contain some kind of fish or shellfish. (Thankfully, dessert escaped this waterbound dictate.) The Catholic Church originally enjoined this meatless meal as a penance, so the body would be cleansed for the feasting that would follow from Christmas Day to Epiphany.

The menu I offer is hardly penitential! It is, however, a sampler of the usual collection of twelve fish dishes, and I have created a fishless vegetable salad. My Italian friends normally serve this menu after midnight mass, so it is designed to be made ahead. Whatever your motive, religious, ethnic, or gustatory, I think you may make it a tradition in your house, too.

Italian Eggplant and Tuna Spread

Spread this tangy mixture on thin slices of Italian bread as an appetizer. Any leftovers can be transformed into an admirable pasta sauce.

2 medium eggplants (about 1 pound each), trimmed, cut into ¾-inch cubes
1 tablespoon plus ½ teaspoon salt, divided
½ cup olive oil
1 large onion, chopped
3 garlic cloves, minced
1 16-ounce can peeled Italian tomatoes, drained and coarsely chopped
1 8-ounce can tomato sauce
3 tablespoons lemon juice
1 tablespoon sugar
1 teaspoon dried basil
¼ teaspoon crushed hot red pepper
2 6½-ounce cans tuna packed in vegetable oil, drained
1 cup pitted green Mediterranean olives, coarsely chopped
¼ cup pine nuts

Sprinkle the eggplants with 1 tablespoon of the salt and let stand in a colander to release their bitter juices, 30 to 60 minutes. Rinse well under cold water and pat dry with paper towels.

In a large skillet, heat 2 tablespoons of the oil over medium heat. Add the onion and cook until softened, about 6 minutes. Add the garlic and stir for 1 minute. Transfer to a bowl and set aside.

In the same skillet, heat 3 tablespoons of the remaining oil. Add half the eggplant and cook over medium heat, stirring often, until lightly browned, about 6 minutes. Transfer to the bowl with the onions and repeat with the remaining oil and eggplant.

Add the tomatoes, tomato sauce, lemon juice, sugar, basil, red pepper, and remaining 1 teaspoon salt, and bring to a simmer over medium heat. Stir in the eggplant mixture and return to a simmer. Cover partially and simmer, stirring often to avoid scorching, until the eggplant is tender, 15 to 20 minutes. Stir in the tuna, olives, and pine nuts and simmer for another 5 minutes.

Transfer to a serving dish and cool to room temperature. Cover and refrigerate for at least 8 hours before serving. Serve the spread at room temperature. (The spread can be made up to 5 days ahead, covered, and refrigerated.)

✘ *Makes about 3½ cups*

Shrimp and Scallop Lasagne with Two Sauces

Everyone loves lasagne, especially when it's lightened up with delectable seafood in this extra-special holiday version. Two sauces—spicy tomato and creamy white wine—combine to complement the chunky scallop, shrimp, and mushroom filling. If you can find fresh spinach lasagne, it will add a colorful, elegant dimension to the dish, but dried-egg lasagne noodles are just fine, too. All the components can be made ahead of time, and the finished lasagne can wait in the refrigerator for up to six hours before baking.

SPICY TOMATO SAUCE

2 tablespoons olive oil
1 small onion, finely chopped
1 garlic clove, minced
1 28-ounce can crushed tomatoes
1 teaspoon dried basil or ¼ cup finely chopped
    fresh basil leaves
¼ teaspoon crushed hot red pepper

WHITE-WINE SAUCE

5 tablespoons unsalted butter
2 shallots or scallions, minced
⅓ cup all-purpose flour
1 cup milk
½ cup dry white wine
½ cup bottled clam juice
¼ teaspoon salt
⅛ teaspoon freshly ground white pepper
Pinch of grated nutmeg
½ cup freshly grated imported Parmesan cheese

SEAFOOD-MUSHROOM FILLING

2 tablespoons olive oil
10 ounces fresh mushrooms, sliced
1 pound medium shrimp, peeled and deveined
1 pound bay scallops (if you have sea scallops, cut
    into ¾-inch pieces)
½ teaspoon salt
⅛ teaspoon freshly ground white pepper

12 ounces fresh spinach lasagne or 9 ounces dried
    egg lasagne noodles
1 tablespoon olive oil
1 cup grated Swiss or Gruyère cheese
Chopped fresh basil for garnish, optional

To make the spicy tomato sauce: Heat the oil in a medium saucepan over medium heat. Add the onion and cook, stirring often, until softened, about 4 minutes. Add the garlic and cook for 1 minute. Stir in the tomatoes, dried basil, and red pepper and bring to a simmer. Reduce the heat to low and simmer until thickened, about 45 minutes. (The tomato sauce can be made up to 3 days ahead, cooled, tightly covered, and refrigerated.)

To make the white-wine sauce: Melt the butter in a heavy-bottomed medium saucepan over low heat. Add the shallots and cook, stirring, until softened, about 2 minutes. Add the flour and let bubble without browning, stirring constantly, about 2 minutes. Whisk in the milk, wine, clam juice, salt, pepper, and nutmeg. Simmer, whisking often, until thickened, about 10 minutes. Remove from the heat and whisk in the Parmesan cheese. (The white sauce can be prepared up to 1 day ahead. Press a piece of plastic wrap directly onto the surface of the sauce to prevent a skin from forming, slashing the wrap in a few places to allow steam to escape. Cool, then refrigerate until ready to use.)

To make the seafood-mushroom filling: Heat the oil in a large skillet over medium-high heat. Add the mushrooms and cook, stirring occasionally, until they have given off their liquid and are browned, about 10 minutes. Increase the heat to high. Add the shrimp, scallops, salt, and pepper and cook, stirring often, just until the shrimp have turned pink, 1 to 2 minutes. Transfer the mixture to a medium bowl and let stand for 10 minutes. Drain off the collected juices from the mixture, and return the juices to the skillet. Boil the juices over high heat until they are reduced to about 2 tablespoons. Stir the reduced juices and white-wine sauce into the seafood-mushroom mixture.

To assemble the lasagne, preheat the oven to 375° F. Lightly butter a 9- by 13-inch baking dish. In a large pot of lightly salted boiling water, cook the fresh spinach lasagne just until supple, 1 to 3 minutes depending on the dryness of the noodles. (If using dried noodles, cook just until *al dente,* 8 to 10 minutes.) Drain, rinse under cold water, and toss with the oil to avoid sticking.

Spread ½ cup of the tomato sauce in the bottom of the prepared pan. Lengthwise, arrange four overlapping strips of the lasagne noodles. (Trim the noodles to fit the pan.) Spread half the filling over the noodles, then top with four more overlapping noodles. Spread with the remaining filling, and top with the remaining noodles. Spread the remaining tomato sauce over the top layer of noodles, then sprinkle with the Gruyère cheese. (The lasagne can be prepared up to 6 hours ahead, covered tightly, and refrigerated.)

Bake, uncovered, until bubbling, about 30 minutes. Let the lasagne stand for 10 minutes. Just before serving, sprinkle with the basil and cut into 12 rectangles.

✖ *Makes 12 servings*

Prosciutto and Parmesan Muffins

This savory version proves that muffins don't always have to be breakfast fare.

2 large eggs
1 cup milk
⅓ cup olive oil
1¼ cups all-purpose flour
¾ cup yellow cornmeal
2 teaspoons baking powder
½ teaspoon baking soda
⅛ teaspoon salt
⅛ teaspoon crushed hot red pepper
2 tablespoons finely chopped fresh parsley
1 cup finely chopped prosciutto or lean ham
     (about 6 ounces)
¼ cup grated Parmesan cheese

Preheat the oven to 400°F. Butter 10 muffin cups.

In a medium bowl, beat the eggs, milk, and olive oil together until well combined.

In another bowl, sift together the flour, cornmeal, baking powder, baking soda, salt, red pepper, and parsley. Fold into the egg mixture and stir until just combined. Stir in the prosciutto and Parmesan just until evenly distributed, but not smooth.

Spoon the mixture into the prepared muffin cups about three-fourths full. Bake in the preheated oven for about 20 minutes, or until well risen and springy to the touch.

Allow the muffins to stand for 5 minutes before turning them out onto a wire rack to cool. Serve warm. (The muffins can be prepared up to 8 hours ahead, then wrapped in foil and reheated in a 400° F. oven for 10 minutes.)

✖ *Makes 10 muffins*

Green, White, and Red Salad with Sundried-Tomato Pesto Dressing

This salad of broccoli, cherry tomatoes, and cauliflower celebrates the colors of the season, as well as Italy's national flag. The sundried-tomato pesto is also wonderful as a dressing for a pasta salad.

1 large head cauliflower, trimmed (about 2 pounds)

1 large head broccoli, stems pared and cut into ½-inch-thick slices, and remainder cut into florets

1 cup sundried tomatoes in oil, drained (about 6 ounces)

2 garlic cloves, chopped

¼ cup red-wine vinegar

2 tablespoons chopped fresh basil or 1 teaspoon dried

¼ teaspoon salt

¼ teaspoon crushed hot red pepper

1 cup olive oil

1 pint cherry tomatoes, halved

In a large saucepan of lightly salted boiling water, cook the whole cauliflower head until just crisp-tender, 5 to 7 minutes. Using two spoons, remove the cauliflower from the water and transfer to a bowl of iced water to cool; drain well. Cut the cauliflower into florets. In the same saucepan, add the broccoli stems and cook for 2 minutes. Add the broccoli florets and continue cooking until the broccoli is just crisp-tender, about an additional 2 minutes. Drain the broccoli, rinse under cold water, and drain again. (The vegetables can be prepared up to 1 day ahead. Wrap the vegetables in paper towels, then place in plastic bags and refrigerate.)

In a food processor fitted with the metal blade or a blender, pulse the sundried tomatoes, garlic, red-wine vinegar, basil, salt, and red pepper until finely chopped. With the machine running, slowly add the oil until thickened. (The dressing can be prepared up to 3 days ahead, covered, and refrigerated.)

In a large salad bowl, arrange the broccoli, cauliflower, and cherry tomatoes, drizzling each layer with some of the dressing. Serve the salad cold or at room temperature.

✗ *Makes about 16 servings*

Amaretto Cheesecake

Here's a delectable version of creamy ricotta cheesecake, made especially distinctive with ground almonds and a dash of almond-flavored liqueur.

1 tablespoon unsalted butter, softened
¾ cup shortbread cookie crumbs (about 4 ounces)
¾ cup whole unskinned almonds (about 3 ounces)
¾ cup sugar
2 pounds whole-milk ricotta cheese
3 large eggs
3 tablespoons almond-flavored liqueur, such as
    Amaretto
¼ teaspoon almond extract

Preheat the oven to 350°F. Coat the inside of a 9-inch-round springform pan with the butter. Sprinkle the bottom and halfway up the sides of the pan with the cookie crumbs. Press the crumbs onto the bottom of the pan. Wrap the outside bottom of the pan tightly with aluminum foil.

In a food processor fitted with the metal blade (or in a blender in batches), process the almonds and sugar until very finely ground. Add the ricotta, eggs, liqueur, and almond extract and pulse until smooth. (The ricotta can also be rubbed through a sieve into a bowl. Add the almond-sugar mixture, eggs, almond liqueur, and extract and mix well with a spoon. Do not mix with an electric mixer, or the batter will aerate, and the cheesecake won't have the proper texture.) Pour the batter into the prepared pan and smooth the top.

Bake until the sides of the cheesecake are puffed and golden brown, 1 hour 15 minutes to 1 hour 30 minutes. (Don't be concerned if the center isn't completely firm.) Run a sharp knife around the inside of the pan to release the cheesecake from the sides. Let cool completely on a wire cake rack in a draft-free place. Cover with plastic wrap and refrigerate until completely chilled, at least 4 hours or overnight.

Remove the sides of the springform pan. Using a knife dipped into hot water between each slice, cut the cheesecake and serve chilled.

✗ *Makes 12 to 16 servings*

Winter Fruit Salad in Grapefruit Cups

Homemade "Everything-in-It" Granola

Scrambled Eggs with Basque Vegetables and Ham

Raspberry Crisp Cake

Hot Coffee   Hot Tea   Hot Chocolate

Chapter Ten

Brunch on Christmas Morning

Some families make a big deal out of Christmas breakfast and others settle for a piece of toast and put all their energies into Christmas dinner. We like to make a big production out of everything: breakfast, dinner, and every opportunity to eat something glorious in between and after. Long walks and no-fault naps are taken as they become necessary.

Christmas breakfast in our house is a feast, although I serve it in the simplest style—pinecones and apples heaped in a strapwork basket are the only decorations on the table—and we sit around it for a couple of hours and sometimes more. In fact, we never seem to finish before noontime, officially qualifying this meal for ''brunch'' status.

Winter Fruit Salad in Grapefruit Cups

Fresh tangerines, grapefruit, and red grapes make a taste-tingling eye-opener. Drizzle each serving with a tablespoon or two of Grand Marnier or crème de cassis if you wish.

4 large grapefruit
2 tangerines, peeled, separated into sections
1½ cups halved red seedless grapes
Fresh mint sprigs, for garnish

Halve the grapefruits horizontally. Using a grapefruit knife, remove the grapefruit flesh. Cut into sections between the membranes. Cut the edges of the grapefruit shells into a zigzag scalloped pattern. In a medium bowl, combine the grapefruit and tangerine sections with the grapes. Spoon into the grapefruit shells, garnish with the mint sprigs, and serve immediately.

✘ *Makes 8 servings*

Homemade "Everything-in-It" Granola

This recipe makes a huge amount of granola, which is good if you expect a big family party for Christmas breakfast. Even if you live alone, you will be surprised how quickly it is finished. It is good with low-fat milk, better with yogurt, and much better with light cream—though admittedly the guilt overcomes the pleasure! You may want to put some in an earthenware or other attractive container and give it to a healthy, or hoping-to-be-healthy, friend.

5 cups rolled (not instant) oats
1 cup raw wheat germ (available at natural-food stores)
½ cup sunflower seeds
1 cup honey or brown sugar
2 cups coarsely chopped pecans
1 cup powdered milk (1 3.2-ounce envelope)
½ cup sesame seeds
1 tablespoon vanilla extract
2 teaspoons salt
1 cup vegetable oil
¼ cup water
1 cup dried apricots, coarsely chopped
1 cup dried apples, coarsely chopped
1 cup dried prunes or dates, pitted and chopped
1 cup dark raisins

Preheat the oven to 250° F. Combine all, or as many of these ingredients as you can put together, in a huge bowl. You will probably have to use your hands to turn the mixture over until it is thoroughly combined. Divide between 2 jelly-roll pans and toast in the preheated oven for 1 hour. Stir the ingredients well every 15 minutes, turning them over to be sure that nothing burns on the bottom.

Remove the pans from the oven and allow the mixture to stand for about 1 hour until it has cooled completely. Pack into apothecary jars, old-fashioned candy jars, or other airtight containers. It keeps indefinitely—or for at least 8 weeks, which is quite a long time.

✘ *Makes about 16 cups*

Left to right: Homemade "Everything-in-It" Granola, Raspberry Crisp Cake, Winter Fruit Salad in Grapefruit Cups

Scrambled Eggs with Basque Vegetables and Ham

The number of eggs may seem excessive when nowadays two eggs are considered sufficient for one person for a year. I have added a few extra not only because they will most certainly be eaten but also because a generous quantity of eggs in a beautiful dish is one of the most comforting sights at the start of a special day.

2 tablespoons olive oil
1 large Bermuda onion, halved and thinly sliced
2 medium green bell peppers, seeded and cut into ¼-inch-wide strips
2 medium red bell peppers, seeded and cut into ¼-inch-wide strips
2 medium yellow bell peppers, seeded and cut into ¼-inch-wide strips
3 garlic cloves, finely chopped
1 box (1 pound) cherry tomatoes, each tomato cut in half
½ pound baked Virginia or other kind of ham without a sweet glaze, cut into thin strips

FOR THE SCRAMBLED EGGS
6 tablespoons (¾ stick) unsalted butter
20 large eggs
½ cup milk
1 teaspoon salt
½ teaspoon freshly ground black pepper
⅓ cup finely chopped fresh chives, optional

Scrambled Eggs with Basque Vegetables and Ham, Homemade "Everything-in-It" Granola

Heat the oil over medium heat in a large skillet. Add the onion and cook until softened, but not browned, about 6 minutes. Stir in the green, red, and yellow bell peppers and garlic. Cook until crisp-tender but still brightly colored, about 8 minutes. (The vegetables can be prepared up to 2 hours ahead of time and set aside at room temperature.)

Add the tomatoes and ham to the skillet and cook over medium-low heat until just warm. Do not overcook—the tomatoes should retain their shape.

To make the scrambled eggs: Heat the butter over medium-low heat in a large flameproof casserole, or in 2 batches, using a very large skillet.

Meanwhile, whisk the eggs, milk, salt, and pepper in a large bowl. Add the chopped chives, if you are using them.

Add the egg mixture to the casserole. Using a spatula or large spoon to stir, slowly scramble the eggs for 8 to 10 minutes, or until they are cooked to your liking.

Arrange the eggs on a warmed serving dish. Form a trough in the middle of the eggs and fill with the warm vegetables and ham.

✖ *Serves 8*

Raspberry Crisp Cake

Here is an interesting coffee cake that tastes like a cross between a shortcake and a crumb cake, with the irresistible tangy flavor of raspberries. I think it will become one of the specialties of your house.

3 cups cake flour
1 cup (2 sticks) unsalted butter, at room
    temperature, cut into small pieces
Grated zest of 1 orange
⅔ cup packed light-brown sugar
1 egg yolk
1½ cups frozen raspberries, partially thawed
    (about 6 ounces)

Put the flour in a bowl. Using a pastry cutter or 2 knives, cut the butter into the flour until the mixture is crumbly. Stir in the orange zest and sugar. Add the egg yolk and mix with a fork to form a soft dough. Wrap the dough in plastic wrap and refrigerate for 30 minutes.

Preheat the oven to 350° F. Butter a 10-inch-round springform cake pan.

Take about two thirds of the dough and crumble it over the cake-pan base in an even layer. (There may be a few small bare spaces but they will blend together as the cake cooks.) Spread the raspberries evenly over this layer. Then crumble the remaining dough over the top. Bake in the preheated oven for 40 to 50 minutes, until crisp and lightly browned.

Remove the cake from the oven and allow it to cool in the pan. Remove the sides from the pan. Serve warm or at room temperature.

✖ *Makes a 10-inch cake; serves 8 to 10*

Left to right: Winter Fruit Salad in Grapefruit Cups, Raspberry Crisp Cake, Homemade "Everything-in-It" Granola

Cream of Chestnut Soup with Prosciutto and Sage

Classic Roast Stuffed Turkey
Sausage and Pecan Stuffing
Cornbread and Oyster Stuffing
Giblet Gravy
Cranberry Relish
Puree of White Winter Vegetables
Creamed Onions in Mustard Sauce
Your Own Recipe for Simply Steamed Green Beans

Flaming Plum Pudding with Hard Sauce
Pumpkin Crème Brûlée

Domaine Chandon Blanc de Noirs Champagne

Chapter Eleven

A Turkey Dinner Extravaganza for Twelve

The most important thing about Christmas dinner is that it must be the same every year. No changes. Even the hour at which everyone gathers around the table must be the same. This is no time for the exercise of democracy. I am in charge.

My mother is English, my father was from Scotland, and my childhood was divided between the two countries. Though I have lived in America for decades now, our Christmas dinner is a re-creation of some of my earliest memories, and my American family indulges me, letting me do it my way, knowing how much this means to me. And, I dearly hope, to them as well. They are kind enough to say that they like things just the way they are and every year they bring their friends to share our Christmas celebration.

This year, as always, our long refectory table will be covered with a heavy white cloth, with two red tartan table runners along the sides. Several years ago, I bought a dozen pewter plates at an auction and I use them as "place plates" because they look handsome on the tartan.

The napkins are rolled inside their scarlet ribbon rings and the place cards are made by hand. The centerpiece is a dramatic arrangement of red candles. There are fat candles, large and small candles, tall tapers and small votive lights, arranged along the length of the table on squares of mirror, and I love to watch their reflections dancing and flickering back from the glass.

Each year, as I set out the foods I serve only at Christmas on that table specially set to receive them, I wonder again how it can be always the same yet subtly different, traditional but amazingly ever-new.

For what we are really celebrating, wherever in the world our families may be, is the joy of being together and the love that grows between us as our families expand.

And as Tiny Tim observed, "God bless us every one."

Cream of Chestnut Soup with Prosciutto and Sage

Here is one of the best of all winter soups—luxurious enough to find a place on your Christmas dinner menu.

2 tablespoons unsalted butter
6 ounces thickly sliced prosciutto, coarsely
    chopped (about 1 cup)
2 medium onions, coarsely chopped
4 celery ribs, coarsely chopped
9 cups homemade chicken stock or canned
    low-sodium broth
2 large boiling potatoes, peeled and cut into
    1-inch pieces (about 12 ounces)
1 16-ounce jar vacuum-packed whole chestnuts
1 tablespoon fresh sage or 1 teaspoon dried
¼ teaspoon salt
¼ teaspoon freshly ground white pepper
½ cup heavy cream
Fresh sage or celery leaves, for garnish

In a large saucepan, melt the butter over low heat. Add the prosciutto, onions, and celery. Cover and cook, stirring occasionally, until the onion is softened, about 10 minutes. Add the chicken stock, potatoes, chestnuts, sage, salt, and pepper and bring to a simmer. Cook, covered, until the potatoes are tender, 20 to 30 minutes.

Using a slotted spoon, transfer the soup solids to a food processor fitted with the metal blade and puree until smooth. Stir the solids back into the saucepan. (The soup can be prepared to this point up to 1 day ahead, cooled to room temperature, covered, and refrigerated.)

When ready to serve, add the cream and reheat gently over low heat. Ladle into soup bowls and garnish each serving with a sage leaf.

Note: Freshly roasted chestnuts can be substituted for the jarred variety. Using a sharp paring knife, cut a shallow X through the flat side of the chestnut, just through the tough peel to reveal the flesh. Bake the chestnuts in a preheated 375° F. oven until they are split open and beginning to brown underneath the peel, 20 to 30 minutes. Remove the peel and inner skin of the chestnuts while still warm. If the chestnuts cool and become difficult to peel, return to the oven for a few minutes to rewarm.

✕ *Makes 12 servings*

Classic Roast Stuffed Turkey

The flourish of the turkey carving ceremony adds greatly to the drama of Christmas dinner. Make a supreme effort to find a fresh turkey. The flavor will be incomparably better than that of one that has been frozen stiff. If you choose a smaller hen turkey (12 pounds and below), allow a full pound per person and roast for about 25 minutes per pound. Larger toms (14 pounds and up) have more meat, so allow ¾ pound per person, and roast at about 20 minutes per pound.

Sausage and Chestnut Stuffing (page 159) or Cornbread and Oyster Stuffing (page 160)
1 fresh turkey, well rinsed and patted dry with paper towels
About 8 tablespoons (1 stick) unsalted butter, softened
1 teaspoon salt, or to taste
¾ teaspoon freshly ground black pepper, or to taste

Preheat the oven to 325° F.

Make the stuffing from one of the recipes that follow and loosely fill the cavity. Do this no more than 1 hour ahead of putting the bird in the oven as the warm, moist environment can quickly become an ideal breeding ground for harmful bacteria. Don't pack the stuffing too tightly because it will expand when it is heated—you don't want it to erupt through the skin. Close the cavity with poultry skewers or trussing string.

Massage the turkey skin all over with the softened butter and sprinkle all over with the salt and pepper. Protect the wing tips from becoming overcooked by wrapping them in oiled foil. Using kitchen twine, tie the wings and legs securely to the bird.

Place the turkey on a rack in a shallow roasting pan and pour in 1 cup of water. Roast the turkey, uncovered, basting occasionally, allowing 20 to 25 minutes to the pound, until the internal temperature reaches 180° to 185° F. (You can check this by inserting a meat thermometer sideways into the thickest part of the thigh, not touching a bone.)

It is extremely important to allow the turkey to rest for at least 20 minutes before carving it. This resting period allows the juices that have risen to the surface to redistribute themselves, moistening all the meat evenly. Tent the bird loosely in aluminum foil to keep it warm.

Meanwhile, put the finishing touches to the Giblet Gravy (page 161) and make sure that the carving knife is well sharpened. When everything is ready, set the bird on a well-warmed platter garnished all around with your favorite steamed vegetables and serve it with pride.

Serves 10 to 14

Sausage and Pecan Stuffing

I can never decide what dressing to make, so I often offer two different varieties. Here's a familiar rendition, with sausage, onion, celery, and herbs, but the apple and pecans lift it from the humdrum. Since only one dressing can stuff the turkey, another will have to be baked on the side in a covered casserole.

1 pound bulk pork sausage

4 tablespoons (½ stick) unsalted butter

1 large onion, finely chopped

4 celery ribs with leaves, finely chopped

1 Granny Smith apple, peeled, cored, and finely chopped

6 cups day-old, firm white bread cubes (about 1 inch square)

2 cups coarsely chopped pecans (about 8 ounces)

2 large eggs, lightly beaten

2 teaspoons dried thyme

2 teaspoons dried sage

1 teaspoon dried rosemary

1 teaspoon salt

¼ teaspoon freshly ground black pepper

½ cup homemade turkey or chicken stock or canned low-sodium chicken broth

In a large skillet, cook the sausage over medium heat, stirring often to break up the sausage, until completely cooked, about 10 minutes. Using a slotted spoon, transfer the cooked sausage to a paper-towel–lined plate to drain, and discard the fat in the skillet. Transfer the drained sausage to a large bowl.

In the same skillet, heat the butter over medium-low heat. Add the onion, celery, and apple. Cover and cook, stirring occasionally, until softened, about 8 minutes. Transfer to the bowl with sausage.

Add the bread cubes, pecans, eggs, thyme, sage, rosemary, salt, and pepper; toss well to combine. Stir in the turkey stock to moisten. Either use as a stuffing or bake separately.

To bake separately, preheat the oven to 350° F. Spread the stuffing in a buttered 13- by 9-inch baking dish and cover with foil. Bake until heated through, about 30 minutes. If you like a crispy top, remove the foil during the last 15 minutes.

✖ *Makes about 7 cups*

Clockwise from left: Cornbread and Oyster Stuffing, Sausage and Pecan Stuffing, Cranberry Relish

Cornbread and Oyster Stuffing

This is very quickly made, using a cornbread stuffing mix as a foundation, and you can double or triple the recipe, as needed.

4 tablespoons (½ stick) unsalted butter
4 medium onions, finely chopped
2 ribs celery, with the leaves, finely chopped
1 sweet red bell pepper, seeded and finely chopped
3 tablespoons finely chopped fresh parsley
1 teaspoon dried oregano
1 16-ounce bag cornbread stuffing
1 cup chicken stock or canned low-sodium broth
2 pints shucked oysters with their liquor

1½ cups frozen corn kernels, thawed
¼ teaspoon cayenne pepper

In a large skillet, melt the butter over medium heat. Add the onion, celery, and bell pepper and cook, stirring occasionally, about 10 minutes, until softened. Transfer to a large bowl and stir in all the remaining ingredients. Fill the turkey with the stuffing.

To bake separately, preheat the oven to 350° F. Spread the stuffing in a buttered 13- by 9-inch baking dish and cover with foil. Bake until heated through, about 30 minutes. If you like a crispy top, remove the foil during the last 15 minutes.

✖ *Makes 8 cups*

Giblet Gravy

This is an absolutely essential part of the feast. I don't include the liver because it makes the gravy cloudy. (In fact, I usually fry the liver up in a little butter and eat it myself, as the cook's treat.)

1 small onion, finely chopped
1 stalk celery, thinly sliced
3 sprigs parsley
Turkey giblets, except the liver, cut into small
    pieces
3 cups homemade chicken stock or canned
    low-sodium broth
2 cups water
4 tablespoons (½ stick) unsalted butter
6 tablespoons all-purpose flour
Salt and freshly ground black pepper, to taste
⅓ cup heavy cream, optional

Put the onion, celery, parsley, and giblets in a medium saucepan. Add the chicken stock and water and simmer, uncovered, for about 1½ hours until the liquid has reduced to 3 cups. Discard the parsley and the bony neck.

Strain the liquid and put the onion, celery, and giblets in the food processor with the steel blade. Add ½ cup of the strained stock and process until very finely chopped. Or, if you prefer, you can chop the onion, celery, and giblets with a sharp knife.

Melt the butter in the medium saucepan over medium heat and stir in the flour. Cook for 2 minutes until the flour is lightly browned. Using a wire whisk, stir in the broth and chopped giblets. Bring to a sim-mer and cook until thickened, about 6 minutes. Season generously with salt and pepper. If you like, you can add the cream, which gives the gravy an appealing color and enriches the flavor still more, but the gravy tastes quite good without it.

✖ *Makes 2 cups*

Cranberry Relish

This relish looks good set out in a glass bowl, but the cranberries take on sensational life in a dark-green, deep-blue, or charcoal-black bowl.

2 cups fresh or frozen cranberries
Grated zest of 1 large navel orange
¼ cup orange juice
1 cup sugar
1 teaspoon ground mustard dissolved in
    1 teaspoon cold water
1 tablespoon cider vinegar

Rinse the cranberries and put them in a heavy saucepan. Add the grated orange zest and juice and the sugar. Bring just to boiling point, then reduce the heat and simmer gently for 5 minutes. Remove from the heat and stir in the dissolved mustard and the vinegar. Cool completely, then cover and refrigerate for at least 24 hours before serving. (The relish can be prepared up to 2 weeks ahead, covered, and refrigerated.)

✖ *Makes about 1½ cups*

Puree of White Winter Vegetables

Richard Olney, one of the most distinguished of all food writers, created the original idea for this superb recipe, which elevates mashed potatoes to an almost celestial plane.

3½ cups homemade chicken stock or canned
   low-sodium broth
3 large yellow onions, finely chopped
3 garlic cloves, finely chopped
2 small turnips, peeled and cut into 1-inch pieces
   (about 8 ounces)
8 medium white boiling (not baking) potatoes,
   peeled and cut into 1-inch pieces
   (about 2½ pounds)
2 bulbs fennel, coarsely chopped (about
   2½ pounds)
2 medium celery roots, pared and cut into 1-inch
   pieces
1 teaspoon salt
¼ teaspoon ground white pepper
⅛ teaspoon ground nutmeg
⅔ cup heavy cream
4 tablespoons (½ stick) unsalted butter
3 tablespoons chopped fresh chives, for garnish

Heat the chicken stock in a large saucepan until simmering. Add all the prepared vegetables, cover, and cook over low heat for 20 to 30 minutes until they are tender. Drain the vegetables and reserve the stock for making soup on another day.

Return the vegetables to the saucepan and add the salt, pepper, and nutmeg. Mash to your desired consistency using a potato masher. Cook over medium-low heat, stirring often, to evaporate any excess moisture. Beat in the cream and butter. Serve immediately, garnished with chopped chives.

✖ *Serves 12*

Creamed Onions in Mustard Sauce

This quantity would not really serve twelve if it were the only side dish on the table, but I am assuming some people will decline, and others will have their plates heaped so high that they will take only a tiny serving. Mustard adds zest to what is traditionally a bland dish. While you may certainly boil fresh white onions, if you wish, I find it more reasonable to use the frozen variety.

2 tablespoons unsalted butter

2 tablespoons all-purpose flour

1½ cups homemade turkey or chicken stock, or canned low-sodium broth

½ cup heavy cream

2 large egg yolks

4 teaspoons Dijon mustard

2 teaspoons lemon juice

⅛ teaspoon salt

⅛ teaspoon freshly ground white pepper

2 1-pound bags frozen small whole white onions

In a medium saucepan, melt the butter over low heat. Whisk in the flour. Let bubble without browning, whisking often, for 2 minutes. Whisk in the stock and heavy cream and bring to a simmer. Cook, whisking often, until thickened, about 5 minutes.

In a small bowl, whisk the egg yolks, Dijon mustard, and lemon juice until combined. Gradually whisk about ½ cup of the hot sauce into the bowl. Return the mixture to the saucepan and cook over low heat, stirring constantly, until the egg yolks have thickened the sauce a little more, about 1 minute. Season the sauce with the salt and white pepper. (The sauce can be prepared up to 1 day ahead, cooled, covered, and refrigerated. Reheat carefully in the top part of a double boiler over simmering water.)

In a large saucepan of lightly salted boiling water, cook the onions until heated through, about 5 minutes. Drain well. Combine the onions with the warm sauce. Transfer to a warmed serving dish and serve immediately.

✗ *Makes about 12 servings*

Flaming Plum Pudding with Hard Sauce

Plum pudding seems never to have contained fresh plums, but rather dried prunes. This version updates the original by using butter instead of the beef suet, which is hard for many of us to get, even from a friendly butcher. Plum pudding is really a sort of steamed fruit cake in which small silver (never copper) charms such as horseshoes, bells, and coins used to be hidden as talismans, bringing good luck to those who found them on their plates. Again, as you will serve a spread of desserts, some of your guests will want just a sliver of pudding so this should stretch to feed a crowd. Steamed pudding molds and glacé citrus rinds can be mail-ordered from Williams-Sonoma, 1-800-541-2233.

PLUM PUDDING

8 tablespoons (1 stick) unsalted butter, softened
1¼ cups packed light-brown sugar
2 large eggs, lightly beaten
⅓ cup plus ¼ cup brandy or dark rum, divided
2 tablespoons unsulfured molassses
2½ cups fresh bread crumbs (made from crustless, firm white bread slices)
½ cup all-purpose flour
¾ cup golden raisins
¾ cup finely chopped pitted prunes
¾ cup currants
¾ cup glacé citrus rinds (use orange rind and/or lemon)
½ cup chopped almonds
1 Granny Smith apple, peeled, cored, and grated
Grated zest of 1 orange
1 teaspoon baking soda
1 teaspoon ground allspice
1 teaspoon ground cinnamon
1 teaspoon ground nutmeg
½ teaspoon ground cloves
½ teaspoon salt

HARD SAUCE
1 cup (2 sticks) unsalted butter, softened
1 cup confectioners' sugar
¼ cup brandy or dark rum

To make the plum pudding: In a large bowl, using a hand-held electric mixer set at high speed, beat the butter until creamy, about 1 minute. Add the sugar and beat until light in color and texture, about 2 more minutes. Beat in the eggs, ⅓ cup of the brandy and the molasses.

In another large bowl, combine all the remaining ingredients and mix well with your hands. Stir in the creamed mixture until smooth.

Butter and flour well the inside of a 2½-quart steamed-pudding mold. Transfer the batter to the prepared mold and attach the lid. Put the mold in a large soup kettle and add enough boiling water to come one fourth of the way up the sides. Cover tightly and simmer over low heat until the pudding is firm, about 3 hours, refilling the kettle with boiling water, if needed. (The plum pudding can be prepared up to 1 day ahead, covered, and refrigerated. Reheat in the kettle of simmering water until heated through, about 45 minutes.)

TO MAKE THE HARD SAUCE: In a medium bowl, using a hand-held electric mixer set at high speed, beat the butter until creamy, about 1 minute. On low speed, beat in the confectioners' sugar until smooth. Beat in the brandy. (The hard sauce can be prepared up to 2 weeks ahead, covered tightly, and refrigerated. Bring to room temperature before serving.)

Pumpkin Crème Brûlée, Flaming Plum Pudding with Hard Sauce

Let the pudding stand for 15 minutes before removing the lid and unmolding onto a serving platter. To flame the pudding, barely heat the remaining ¼ cup of brandy in a small saucepan over low heat. At the table, strike a match, carefully ignite the brandy, and pour it over the pudding. Slice the pudding and serve warm with the hard sauce.

✗ *Makes 8 to 12 servings*

✗ *Makes 2 cups Hard Sauce*

The Zen of Christmas Pudding

- The round, dark pudding represents the good and abundant earth.
- The red berries on the sprig of holly symbolize the blood of Christ. (Even though holly sprigs are a traditional garnish for plum pudding, remember that both the leaves and berries are poisonous. You may want to take the opportunity to use pretty plastic holly.)
- The brandy flames stand for the fires of hell, which are burned away as goodness triumphs over evil.

The tradition of making plum pudding goes back for centuries. In England, the Sunday before Advent Sunday used to be known as Stir-up Sunday, because the prayer for that day began "Stir up, we beseech Thee, O Lord, the wills of thy faithful people"—and on that day everybody started making (and stirring up) the puddings to be served at Christmas. For good luck, the pudding mixture had to be stirred always in a clockwise direction, every member of the family had to take a turn with the spoon, and everyone made a wish—but never revealed it, of course, or it would not come true.

Pumpkin Crème Brûlée

A lighter version of that holiday perennial, pumpkin pie, this smooth-as-silk custard has a crisp broiled-sugar topping. Make the custards a day or two ahead, then broil the toppings just before serving.

1 29-ounce can pumpkin puree
1½ cups sugar
6 large eggs
2 teaspoons ground cinnamon
1 teaspoon ground ginger
1 teaspoon ground nutmeg
2 cups heavy cream, scalded
½ cup packed light brown sugar

Preheat the oven to 325° F. In a large bowl, whisk together the pumpkin, sugar, eggs, cinnamon, ginger, and nutmeg. Gradually whisk in the scalded cream until smooth. Divide the mixture evenly among twelve 5- to 6-ounce custard cups.

Place the custard cups in baking pans, and add enough hot water to come ½ inch up the sides. Bake until a knife inserted in the center of a custard comes out clean, about 45 minutes. Cool the custards completely. Cover each custard with plastic wrap, then refrigerate until cold, at least 4 hours or overnight. (The custards can be prepared up to 2 days ahead, covered, and refrigerated.)

Position the rack about 4 inches from the source of heat and preheat the broiler. Place the custards close together on a baking sheet. Force the brown sugar through a coarse sieve, allowing the sugar to fall directly on the tops. Place the sheet of custards in the broiler and broil until the sugar is melted, watching carefully to be sure the sugar doesn't burn, about 2 minutes. Serve the custards immediately, or refrigerate until ready to serve, up to 1 day.

Note: The custard can also be prepared in two round 1½-quart baking dishes. Place each baking dish in a larger baking pan and add enough hot water to come ½ inch up the sides. Bake until a knife inserted in the center of the custards comes out clean, about 1 hour 45 minutes. When ready to broil the topping, use about ¼ cup of the sugar on each custard.

✕ *Makes 12 servings*

Fresh Oysters with Balsamic Mignonette Sauce

Winter Tomato Consommé

Pear and Red Wine Sorbet

Prime Ribs of Beef au Poivre with Cognac au Jus
Scalloped Celery Root, Potato, and Garlic
Haricot Verts, Wild Mushrooms, and Shallots
Celebration Baked Alaska (with Butter Pound Cake)

An Assortment of Cheeses

Chardonnay   Cabernet Sauvignon   Champagne

Chapter Twelve

A Fancy Prime Rib Dinner for Eight

The holidays are a lovely excuse to stage a proper fancy dinner complete with all the excesses and flourishes the genre demands. Create the mood with an astonishing array of your best tableware—lots of gleaming, carefully polished silver, rows of glistening crystal glasses, the finest china, the crispest linen.

A complex dinner requires a certain sense of orchestration. If it is planned properly, you can calmly serve a surfeit of courses with assurance. The first three courses can be prepared well ahead and need only be served up when required. Begin with a light but elegant first course of fresh oysters with a balsamic vinegar sauce. Then segue into a refreshingly simple tomato consommé, again teasing your guests' palates without ruining their appetites. As this is a black-tie affair, a sorbet course is appropriate, such as the pear and red wine sorbet offered here.

For the main course, choose a spectacular main dish that denotes luxury and plenitude, such as a magnificent prime-rib roast encrusted with peppercorns in a cognac sauce. The side dishes are a lovely celery-root gratin and tiny green beans sautéed with wild mushrooms. Depending on your guests' constitutions, you may choose to serve a simple green salad vinaigrette before dessert, or perhaps pass perfectly ripened cheese and fruits. But remember that you are serving the grandest finale a dinner can ask for—Baked Alaska—so, for once during the holidays, restraint may be more admirable than indulgence.

Fresh Oysters with Balsamic Mignonette Sauce

Plump, fresh oysters are a superlative taste-teaser at formal dinners where subsequent courses promise to be rich and indulgent. The complex, slightly sweet flavor of balsamic vinegar is a nice counterpoint to the saltiness of the shellfish.

½ cup balsamic vinegar
2 shallots, finely minced
1 tablespoon fresh tarragon or 1 teaspoon dried
⅛ teaspoon freshly ground pepper
32 fresh oysters, freshly opened

Mix the vinegar, shallots, tarragon, and pepper and divide among eight small bowls. Arrange the oysters on eight individual serving dishes, and serve immediately, providing each guest with a bowl of the vinegar dip.

✕ *Makes 8 servings*

Winter Tomato Consommé

This is the easiest of soups to make, and my guests always enjoy its full-bodied flavor with an unfilling profile. I like to garnish it with a swirl of basil pesto, but feel free to use Coriander and Pumpkin Seed Pesto (page 10) for added zip.

6 cups homemade chicken stock or canned
      low-sodium broth
4 cups tomato juice
1 cup finely chopped shallots or scallions
2 teaspoons tomato paste
½ teaspoon dried thyme
½ teaspoon dried basil

½ teaspoon ground allspice
2 teaspoons lemon juice
2 tablespoons dry sherry
2 tablespoons finely chopped fresh chives
      or fresh parsley
½ cup Classic Basil Pesto (page 11)

Combine the stock, tomato juice, shallots or scallions, tomato paste, thyme, basil, and allspice in a saucepan. Gently simmer the soup, over low heat, for 15 minutes. Strain. Stir in the lemon juice, sherry, and chives and reheat just until hot.

Garnish each serving with a dollop of the pesto and serve immediately.

✗ *Serves 8*

Pear and Red Wine Sorbet

This sophisticated sorbet is at its best eaten within 24 hours. It will not become very firm because of the relatively large amount of alcohol it contains.

2 cups sugar
4 cups red wine
3 tablespoons lemon juice
6 fresh Anjou pears, peeled, cored, and halved (about 2½ pounds)
¼ cup pear brandy (preferably Poire William)

Combine the sugar, red wine, and lemon juice in a saucepan and bring to boiling point over high heat, stirring constantly to dissolve the sugar. Reduce the heat to very low and simmer for 5 minutes.

Add the pear halves to the pan and simmer for 15 to 20 minutes, until the pears are tender. Remove from the heat and cool to room temperature. Spoon the pears with some of the wine syrup into a blender or food processor and puree until smooth. Add the remaining wine syrup and the brandy and blend again. Chill the mixture.

Freeze in an ice-cream maker according to the manufacturer's directions. The mixture will not freeze solid. Transfer to a metal bowl, cover tightly, and freeze at least 6 hours before serving.

✘ *Makes about 1½ quarts*

Prime Ribs of Beef au Poivre with Cognac au Jus

Steak au poivre is one of the most popular of French bistro entrées. Prime ribs of beef, an impressive and glorious addition to the holiday table, gets the "au poivre" treatment with a crust of crushed mixed peppercorns and a cognac-enhanced serving sauce.

1 7- to 8-pound four-rib prime rib roast
3 garlic cloves, peeled
1 tablespoon coarse (kosher) salt
3 tablespoons mixed peppercorns (black, white, pink, and dried green, or any combination), crushed
1 tablespoon vegetable oil
3 shallots, minced
¼ cup cognac
1½ cups unsalted beef stock or canned unsalted broth
Salt and freshly ground black pepper, to taste

Using a sharp knife, cut off the fat "cap" from the roast in one piece. Cut just where the fat is attached to the meat, trimming off as little meat as possible. Reserve the fat "cap."

On a work surface, sprinkle the garlic with the salt. Crush and smear the garlic while chopping to create a garlic paste. In a small bowl, combine the garlic paste and peppercorns. Brush the top of the roast with the oil. Spread the peppercorn paste on the top of the roast, pressing it into the roast with the heel of your hand. Replace the fat cap and tie it back onto the roast with kitchen twine. (The roast can be prepared up to 1 day ahead, covered loosely with plastic wrap, and refrigerated.)

Preheat the oven to 500° F. Place the roast, fat side up without a rack, in a large roasting pan. Roast for 15 minutes. Reduce the heat to 325° F., and continue roasting for about 17 minutes a pound (including the first 15-minute period) for medium-rare meat, until a meat thermometer inserted in the thickest part of the roast reads 130° F., about 2½ hours for an 8-pound roast. Remove the roast from the pan and transfer to a carving board. Let stand at least 15 minutes before slicing.

Meanwhile, pour off all but 1 tablespoon of the fat in the pan. Place the pan on top of the stove over medium heat. Add the shallots and cook, stirring, until softened, about 1 minute. Add the cognac. Averting your face, light the cognac with a match, let burn for 10 seconds, then extinguish the flame by covering with the lid of the pan. Add the beef stock and cook until the liquid is reduced to about 1 cup, 8 to 10 minutes. Transfer to a glass measuring cup and let stand 5 minutes. Skim off any fat that rises to the surface, and pour into a warmed sauceboat.

Discard the kitchen twine. Remove the fat cap to reveal the peppercorn crust. (In spite of what their doctors have told them, there will be guests who crave a taste of the roasted fat, so don't be so heartless as to discard it.) Carve the roast and serve with the sauce on the side.

✖ *Makes 8 servings*

Scalloped Celery Root, Potato, and Garlic

Everyone loves scalloped potatoes with roast beef. My rendition gets a lift from celery root and garlic. I always like to parboil the potatoes and celery root before baking, as it takes some of the guesswork out of the cooking time. (No one likes raw scalloped potatoes, and I have spent more than a few nervous moments in the kitchen waiting for the darned things to cook all the way through.)

3 tablespoons unsalted butter, softened and
    divided
3 garlic cloves, minced
5 large baking potatoes, peeled and cut into
    ⅛-inch-thick slices (about 2½ pounds)
2 large celery roots, pared, halved, and cut into
    ⅛-inch-thick slices (about 2½ pounds)
2 cups heavy cream, scalded and hot
¾ teaspoon salt
¼ teaspoon freshly ground white pepper

Preheat the oven to 400° F. Butter a 9- by 13-inch baking dish with 1 tablespoon of the butter. Sprinkle the dish with the garlic. Add the potatoes and celery roots to a large saucepan of lightly salted boiling water. Return to the boil and parboil for 2 minutes (the vegetables will not be cooked). Drain well.

Spread the par-cooked vegetables in the prepared pan. Pour in the hot cream and season with the salt and pepper. Dot with the remaining butter. Bake until the top is golden brown and the cream is evaporated, 50 to 60 minutes. Serve immediately.

✂ *Makes 8 servings*

Haricots Verts, Wild Mushrooms, and Shallots

Even if you can't find the delicate, slender haricots verts, or the earthy wild mushrooms, or the aromatic shallots—make this elegant side dish with the suggested substitutions. This is a superlative dish served with turkey, as well.

1 pound haricots verts (tiny green beans), trimmed, or 1½ pounds green beans, trimmed and cut into 1-inch lengths

4 tablespoons (½ stick) unsalted butter, divided

2 shallots or scallions, finely chopped

1 pound wild mushrooms (such as cremini or stemmed shiitake), sliced, or white button mushrooms

2 teaspoons chopped fresh thyme leaves or ½ teaspoon dried

½ teaspoon salt

¼ teaspoon pepper

In a large saucepan of lightly salted boiling water, cook the haricots verts just until crisp-tender, about 3 minutes. Drain, rinse under cold water, and drain again. (The haricots verts can be prepared up to 1 day ahead, wrapped in paper towels, placed in a plastic bag, and refrigerated.)

In a large skillet, heat 2 tablespoons of the butter over medium heat. Add the shallots and cook, stirring, until softened, about 2 minutes. Add the mushrooms and cook, stirring often, until the mushrooms have given off their liquid and are beginning to brown,

about 8 minutes. (The dish can be prepared up to this point about 3 hours ahead of serving and left at room temperature. Reheat to sizzling before proceeding.)

Add the haricots verts, thyme, salt, and pepper. Cook, stirring often, until the haricots verts are heated through, about 5 minutes. Stir in the remaining 2 tablespoons of butter. Transfer to a warmed serving dish and serve immediately.

✗ *Makes 8 servings*

Celebration Baked Alaska

Baked Alaska is about as dramatic a dessert as there ever was. Use Butter Pound Cake (page 181) if you like, though a store-bought pound cake makes an excellent base for the Alaska—it has just the firm texture that is required. I am never content to leave well enough alone, so I enjoy heightening the drama of the presentation by sinking the empty eggshell halves into the baked meringue and filling them with warmed brandy. Light the brandy at the table.

1 pound cake (9 by 5 inches), either homemade or
    store-bought
1 cup fresh or frozen raspberries
4 large egg whites (reserve 2 of the eggshell
    halves)
$\frac{1}{8}$ teaspoon cream of tartar
$\frac{2}{3}$ cup granulated sugar
1 pint vanilla ice cream, softened just enough to
    be easily spooned
3 tablespoons brandy, heated

Preheat the oven to 425° F.

Cut the cake lengthwise into thick slices. On a sheet of parchment paper, arrange the cake slices, trimming as necessary, to make a rectangle about 9 inches long.

(Reserve the cake trimmings for another use.) Spread a layer of raspberries over the cake.

To make the meringue, put the egg whites into the large mixing bowl of an electric mixer. Add the cream of tartar. Beat at the highest speed until the egg whites stand in soft peaks. Beat in the sugar gradually and continue beating until the mixture stands in stiff peaks. Transfer the meringue to a pastry bag fitted with a large decorating star tip, such as Ateco Number 5.

Cover the fruit-topped cake with softened ice cream. Pipe the meringue over the ice cream and cake, taking great care to cover the ice cream completely. Or you may simply spead the meringue over the ice cream with a rubber spatula. (The meringue will insulate the ice cream and momentarily prevent it from melting when it enters the hot oven.) Bake in the preheated oven for about 4 to 5 minutes until the meringue is lightly browned.

Using a wide metal spatula, slide the baked Alaska onto a serving dish. Trim off the excess parchment paper with scissors. Sink the eggshells into the meringue, working quickly. Warm the brandy in a very small saucepan and pour it carefully into the eggshells. Light the brandy at the table, using a nice-looking long match—not a guest's Zippo cigarette lighter. Serve immediately.

✕ *Serves 8*

Butter Pound Cake

For those in the crowd who want a homemade pound cake in the freezer to use in various guises throughout the season, here's the classic version. I use a thick horizontal slice of it for my Celebration Baked Alaska. Use any leftovers in your favorite trifle recipe, or spoon warmed mincemeat over cake slices for a quick dessert.

1 cup (2 sticks) unsalted butter, softened
1 cup sugar
5 large eggs, at room temperature
½ teaspoon vanilla extract
2 cups all-purpose flour
1 teaspoon baking powder
½ teaspoon salt

Preheat the oven to 325° F. Butter and flour a 9- by 5-inch loaf pan.

In a large bowl, using a hand-held electric mixer set at high speed, beat the butter until creamy, about 1 minute. Add the sugar and beat until light in color and texture, about 2 minutes. One at a time, beat in the eggs, beating well after each addition. Beat in the vanilla.

Sift together the flour, baking powder, and salt. Using a wooden spoon, stir the flour mixture into the butter mixture. Transfer to the prepared pan and smooth the top.

Bake until golden brown and a toothpick inserted into the center comes out clean, about 60 minutes. Cool in the pan for 10 minutes, then turn out onto a wire cake rack to cool completely. (The cake will keep for 2 days, wrapped tightly in plastic wrap and stored at room temperature. Or, wrap the cake tightly in plastic wrap and then aluminum foil, and freeze for up to 1 month.)

✖ *Makes 1 9-inch loaf*

An Assortment of Cheeses

The key to a fine cheese platter is *variety*. Choose contrasting cheeses of different textures, flavors, shapes, and colors, and the palate, as well as the eye, will be pleased. Selecting cheeses made from different kinds of milk (raw or cooked cow's milk, goat or sheep) will also add zest to your presentation.

Cheeses are often grouped by texture: hard, firm, semisoft, and soft. *Hard* cheeses (such as Parmigiano-Reggiano) have the lowest moisture content and are often used for grating. They can be quite salty, and are not always appropriate to serve as part of your cheese course. There is a huge variety of sharp-flavored *firm* cheeses. These include Cheddar, Cantal, and Gruyère.

The blue-veined cheeses also fall into this category—Roquefort, Blue de Gex, and Shropshire. *Semisoft* cheeses often have the buttery smoothness and thick rinds we identify with Camembert or Brie. Other semisoft cheeses would be Faux Vacherin, Brin d'Amour (a herb-encrusted sheep's cheese from Corsica), Bel Paese and the wreath-shaped Saint Nectaire. *Soft* cheeses are all unctuous in body but can vary in taste from the tangy goat's milk Chevres to the creamy L'Explorateur. Chevres come in a huge array of shapes and flavors. Therefore, I'll often choose two contrasting kinds, such as the pyramid-shaped Chabis (sometimes sprinkled with pink peppercorns and herbs and drizzled with olive oil), and the log-shaped Montrachet, which can be found coated in wood ashes, which give it a gray coating.

Globe Artichokes with House Dressing

Baked Smoked Ham with Apple Cider Glaze

Braised Red Cabbage with Pears

Oven-Roasted Sweet Potatoes

Cottage Cheese and Dill Muffins

Mincemeat Pie with Leaf Crust

Hard Apple Cider or Alsatian Gewürztraminer

Chapter Thirteen

A Home-Style Dinner for Twelve

When planning the menu for a large group of people, you often find that grand schemes can fall by the wayside. Sometimes an uncomplicated approach with lots of down-home flavors is the best way to go.

Again, this menu is full of make-ahead dishes. My California friends tell me that they often start their Christmas meals with my favorite vegetable, a simply boiled artichoke with a delectable vinaigrette dressing. Long-braised red cabbage with pears and the cottage cheese and dill muffins can be prepared in the morning and reheated. Of course, if you serve the gorgeous

mincemeat pie with its crown of pastry leaves, you must begin well in advance, as the mincemeat must age for at least a couple of weeks.

The centerpiece of the meal is an all-time family favorite, a glazed smoked ham. Don't even consider sullying this ham with garish pineapple rings or maraschino cherries—it is basted with apple cider, and that is all you need to do. Served with a simple roast of sweet-potato chunks, it is a cost-wise meal that everyone will enjoy.

Globe Artichokes with House Dressing

I adore artichokes so much that I use one as my company logo! Fortunately, they are at their best in the winter and it is always worth preparing a larger quantity because they keep well in the refrigerator, covered with plastic wrap, and you can serve them again and again. This method of preparing the artichokes gives you a natural receptacle to hold the dressing.

12 medium globe artichokes (about 9 ounces each)
7 to 8 quarts water
1 tablespoon salt
Juice of ½ lemon
My Own Dipping Sauce (see below)

Cut off the artichoke stems so that the artichokes will stand without tipping over. Discard the lowest row of leaves. Lay the artichokes on their sides and cut off ½ inch from the top of each one. Then trim ½ inch from the tip of each leaf, using a pair of sharp scissors.

In a very large saucepan or stockpot, bring the water to a full boil over high heat; add the salt and lemon juice. Add the artichokes and cover the pot. Reduce the heat to low and cook for 30 to 40 minutes. Test for doneness by pulling out a leaf from one of the artichokes; if it comes away easily, they are ready.

Remove the artichokes from the water, using tongs, and set them upside down to drain on paper towels spread over a wire rack; when they are cool enough to handle, squeeze each one gently upside down to remove all the water. Allow to cool completely. One artichoke at a time, pull out the inner core of pale green leaves, revealing the thistle. Using a teaspoon, scoop out the hairy thistle, revealing the artichoke bottom and forming a cavity to hold the dressing.

Combine all the ingredients for My Own Dipping Sauce and pour it into the artichoke cavities. Don't forget to provide bowls for the leaves.

✗ *Serves 12*

....

My Own Dipping Sauce

More guests have asked for this recipe than for any other, and I am always happy to share it.

½ teaspoon salt
¼ teaspoon freshly ground black pepper
3 cloves garlic, finely chopped
2 teaspoons Dijon mustard
½ cup red-wine vinegar
1½ cups olive oil
⅓ cup finely chopped parsley
⅓ cup finely chopped chives, preferably fresh
3 tablespoons finely chopped capers
3 tablespoons finely chopped sweet gherkins
2 hard-cooked large eggs, finely chopped

In a blender, pulse the salt, pepper, garlic, mustard, and vinegar to combine. With the machine running, gradually add the olive oil. Add the parsley, chives, capers, gherkins, and chopped egg and pulse until mixed. (The dressing can be prepared up to 2 days ahead, covered, and refrigerated.)

✗ *Makes 3 cups*

Globe Artichokes with House Dressing, Braised Red Cabbage with Pears

Baked Smoked Ham with Apple Cider Glaze

Quite often, the simplest things are the best. Here, a bone-in smoked ham is basted with apple cider while it bakes, and the cider creates a marvelous glaze. That's it!

1 6-pound bone-in smoked ham, skin scored in a
    diamond pattern
3 cups fresh-pressed apple cider

Preheat the oven to 325° F. Place the ham on a rack in a roasting pan. Pour the apple cider over the ham.

Bake, basting every half hour with the cider, until a meat thermometer inserted in the ham reads 160°F. and the ham is glazed, about 20 minutes per pound. A 6-pound ham will take about 2 hours.

Transfer the ham to a carving board and let stand for 5 minutes before carving. If desired, skim the fat from the surface of the juices and serve the juices with the carved ham.

✗ *Serves 8 to 10*

Clockwise from top left: Cottage Cheese and Dill Muffins, Oven-Roasted Sweet Potatoes, Globe Artichokes with House Dressing, Braised Red Cabbage with Pears, Baked Smoked Ham with Apple Cider Glaze

Braised Red Cabbage with Pears

There's nothing like the tang of sweet and sour cabbage to offset the flavor of smoked pork dishes. Of course, if you make this a day ahead and let it mellow, it will only be that much better.

½ cup packed light-brown sugar
7 tablespoons cider vinegar
½ teaspoon dried thyme
1 bay leaf
¾ teaspoon salt
¼ teaspoon pepper
4 pounds red cabbage, cored and finely shredded
3 large Bosc pears, peeled, cored, and cut into
    ½-inch pieces
½ cup raisins

In a large saucepan, combine the brown sugar, cider vinegar, thyme, bay leaf, salt, and pepper. Bring to a boil over medium-high heat, stirring to dissolve the sugar. In thirds, stir the cabbage into the saucepan, covering the saucepan and letting each batch wilt before adding the next. Stir in the pears and raisins.

Reduce the heat to medium-low and simmer, covered, until the cabbage is very tender, 50 to 60 minutes. Transfer to a warmed serving dish and serve immediately. (The cabbage can be prepared up to 2 days ahead, covered, and refrigerated. Reheat slowly before serving.)

✗ *Makes 12 servings*

Oven-Roasted Sweet Potatoes

Creamy-colored sweet potatoes (or the more common Louisiana yams, which are dark orange and sweeter) are actually best in straightforward preparations, and not gunked up with lots of brown sugar and marshmallows. Try this easy recipe, and you'll be a convert to the "no-frills" method.

6 medium sweet potatoes, peeled and cut into
    1-inch pieces (about 3 pounds)
3 tablespoons unsalted butter
3 tablespoons vegetable oil
¾ teaspoon salt
¼ teaspoon pepper

In a large saucepan of lightly salted boiling water, parboil the sweet potatoes for 5 minutes. Drain, rinse well under cold water, and drain again. (The sweet potatoes can be parboiled up to 1 day ahead, covered, and refrigerated.) Pat the sweet potatoes dry with paper towels.

Position a rack in the top third of the oven and preheat to 400° F. In a large baking dish that will accommodate the sweet potatoes in one layer, combine the butter and vegetable oil. Place the baking dish in the oven until the butter is melted and sizzling, about 3 minutes. Add the sweet potatoes, salt, and pepper and toss to coat.

Bake, stirring occasionally, until the sweet potatoes are golden brown and tender, 50 to 70 minutes. (The exact cooking time depends on the age of the sweet potatoes; the older specimens will be drier.) Serve immediately.

✖ *Makes 8 servings*

Cottage Cheese and Dill Muffins

Here is a muffin change of pace—pleasantly aromatic and not sweet at all.

1 cup all-purpose flour
1 cup quick-cooking rolled oats
1 teaspoon baking powder
½ teaspoon baking soda
½ teaspoon salt
¼ teaspoon freshly ground black pepper
¾ cup low-fat cottage cheese
1 egg, lightly beaten
2 tablespoons milk
⅓ cup vegetable oil
1 tablespoon chopped fresh dill or ¼ teaspoon
    dried

Preheat the oven to 400° F. Butter 10 muffin cups.

Mix the flour, oats, baking powder, baking soda, salt, and pepper in a large bowl. In a second bowl, combine the cottage cheese, egg, milk, oil, and dill. Add this to the flour mixture. Stir until just combined.

Spoon the mixture into the prepared muffin cups about three fourths full. Bake in the preheated oven for 18 to 20 minutes, or until well risen and springy to the touch.

Allow the muffins to stand for 5 minutes before turning them out. Serve warm.

✖ *Makes 10 muffins*

Left to right: Cottage Cheese and Dill Muffins, Baked Smoked Ham with Apple Cider Glaze, Oven-Roasted Sweet Potatoes

Mincemeat Pie
with Leaf Crust

You've aged your Apple-Brandy Mincemeat properly, and the time has come to turn it into that holiday masterpiece, mincemeat pie. Instead of simply topping the pie with the familiar lattice crust, cut the same dough into leaf shapes, and arrange them on top of the mincemeat in a gorgeous spray. You may serve your warm mincemeat pie with Hard Sauce (see page 165), but also try it à la mode, with vanilla or rum-raisin ice cream.

2⅔ cups all-purpose flour

1 teaspoon salt

4 tablespoons (½ stick) unsalted butter, chilled
     and cut into ½-inch pieces

¾ cup vegetable shortening, chilled

½ cup ice water, approximately

4 cups Apple-Brandy Mincemeat (page 195)

1 egg yolk

1 tablespoon heavy cream

In a medium bowl, stir the flour and salt together. Using a pastry blender or two knives, cut the butter into the flour until it resembles small peas. Add the vege-table shortening and blend until the mixture resembles coarse meal. Stirring with a fork, gradually add enough water until the dough holds together when pinched between the thumb and forefinger. (You may have to add more water.) Gather the dough up into a two flat, thick disks and wrap each tightly in waxed paper. Refrigerate until chilled, at least 1 hour or overnight.

Preheat the oven to 375° F. On a lightly floured work surface, roll out one disk to a circle, about 12 inches wide and ⅛ inch thick. Transfer the dough to a 10-inch-round pie plate. Fold the excess dough over into the plate to form a thick rope around the top edge of the plate, then flute the rope decoratively. Spoon the mincemeat into the dough-lined plate. Roll out the remaining dough and cut into leaf shapes. Using the tip of a small knife, mark the leaves with veins. Place the leaves on top of the mincemeat in an attractive pattern.

In a small bowl, mix the yolk and cream together. Brush the leaves and crust lightly with some of yolk mixture. Place the pie plate on a baking sheet. Bake until the leaves are golden brown and the mincemeat is gently bubbling, 35 to 40 minutes. Serve the mincemeat pie hot, warm, or at room temperature.

✄ *Serves 12*

Apple-Brandy Mincemeat

One rarely finds the "meat" in mincemeat anymore. This version substitutes melted butter for the traditional ground beef and suet. (With such a heady combination of ingredients, they added more texture than flavor, and won't be missed at all.) This recipe makes enough for two 9- or 10-inch pies, but do think ahead and let the mincemeat age for at least two weeks for the fullest flavor.

2 cups dark raisins

2 cups currants

1 cup chopped glacé fruits

1 cup fresh bread crumbs

1 cup apple brandy (such as applejack or
    Calvados)

8 tablespoons (1 stick) unsalted butter, melted

½ cup packed light-brown sugar

½ cup chopped slivered almonds

½ cup apricot preserves

2 Granny Smith apples, peeled, cored, and grated

Grated zest and juice of 1 lemon

1 teaspoon ground cinnamon

1 teaspoon ground allspice

1 teaspoon almond extract

½ teaspoon grated nutmeg

½ teaspoon ground cloves

¼ teaspoon salt

Port wine or dark rum, optional

Combine all the ingredients (except the port wine or rum) in large bowl and mix well. Transfer the mixture to hot, sterilized jars or a crock with a lid. Cover and let stand for at least 2 weeks and up to 3 months in a cool, dark place. (The refrigerator is fine.) Stir the mixture once a week. If the mincemeat seems dry upon standing, moisten it with port wine or dark rum, or additional apple brandy.

✖ *Makes about 2 quarts*

Caviar for Two

Salt-Roasted Cornish Hens
Louisiana Rice
Minted Baby Carrots and Sugar Snap Peas

Boston Lettuce and Radicchio Salad
with Roquefort and Pears

Clementines and Raspberries in Grand Marnier

An Extravagant Champagne

Chapter Fourteen

A Romantic Dinner for Two

With some careful planning, there will come a delicious moment during the holidays that is just for two people to be alone together.

This menu has been chosen with great care so that all the cooking can be done without fuss at your own pace. As its price makes it prohibitive in great quantities, I wait for the holidays to indulge in the best caviar with my closest friend. Perhaps it is so expensive because it is so easy to serve. The unusual salt-roasted game hens will be a conversation piece, I guarantee, garnished with a Louisiana-inspired rice dish and baby carrots with sugar snap peas. As this kind of meal should be leisurely, I have included a green salad with Roquefort and pears so you can linger before a simple dessert of chilled oranges and raspberries splashed with Grand Marnier and champagne.

A romantic dinner should be enjoyed under the most sensuous circumstances you can design, remembering that there is still dinner to serve. This is another time to bring out the best china and finest glasses, and to polish the silver so it will gleam in the soft glow of candlelight. Choose a simple centerpiece for the table that will have a special significance to the two of you. When in doubt, a single red rose in a bud vase speaks volumes.

Remember, too, that this menu does not have to be overtly romantic. Cherish a friend, or invite someone you love unromantically to share a quiet meal and Christmas memories. Cooking a meal for someone you love may well be the nicest gift you can give.

Caviar for Two

It's no mere coincidence that caviar is a popular holiday luxury. Like other select commodities, caviar has a season. As the fish eggs are highly perishable, and a fresh harvest comes on the market in December, they are at their absolute best during the early winter months.

The imported caviar from Caspian Sea sturgeon is the finest, but you may also be able to find acceptable American caviar. There are three major common varieties of Caspian caviar: *Beluga* caviar is considered by many to be the top of the line, consisting of large, firm eggs with a mild saline flavor. *Osetra* "berries" (what professionals call the eggs) are slightly smaller, so usually slightly cheaper. *Sevruga* caviar are smaller still, but its flavor is the most pronounced, so it has many aficionados. As free tasting samples are rarely offered at a caviar shop, and you have acquired a preference, let your pocketbook make the choice, and simply buy the best caviar you can. We are discussing *fresh* caviar, not the dyed fish eggs one often finds in jars in the supermarket.

Always buy your caviar from a reputable source. If your city doesn't have a gourmet shop that carries caviar—and sells lots of it, assuring freshness—you may order by phone from Caviar Direct (718-402-6900 or 800-472-4456). It's difficult to estimate exactly how much of the rich, filling caviar to serve, but a little less than one ounce per person as an appetizer portion seems sufficient.

Serve caviar ice cold, preferably in a caviar *servior*, but it can be placed in a bowl and nestled in cracked ice as well. Tradition dictates that caviar is never to be served with a metal spoon, as the metal may react with the taste of the berries. Therefore, bone, wood, or ivory spoons are available, but I have been known to use, for lack of something more elegant, Bakelite or even plastic serving utensils. You may extend your precious portion of caviar by serving it with such accoutrements as toasted bread, minced onion or chives, sour cream or crème frâiche, finely chopped hard-boiled egg yolks and whites, and, of course, wedges of fresh lemon. But please remember not to heap your serving with toppings and turn it into a caviar "sundae." The toppings are meant to enhance, not overwhelm, the delicate morsels.

Salt-Roasted Cornish Hens

Surely one of the most unusual ways to cook poultry, and one that will win praise from your significant other. The hot salt sears the Cornish hens, and the birds retain all their marvelous juices.

1 3-pound box kosher (coarse) salt
2 1¼-pound Cornish game hens, giblets removed
4 garlic cloves, crushed
1 teaspoon freshly ground black pepper
¼ cup vegetable oil

Preheat the oven to 350° F. In a flameproof casserole with a lid, just large enough to hold the hens, place the salt. Cook the salt on top of the stove over medium-high heat, stirring often, until very hot, about 15 minutes.

Meanwhile, rinse the hens and pat dry with paper towels. Place 2 garlic cloves in the body cavity of each hen, and sprinkle each with ½ teaspoon of the pepper. Soak two pieces of cheesecloth (each about 16 inches square) in the oil. Completely wrap each hen in a cheesecloth square.

When the salt is hot, pour almost all of it out into a heatproof bowl, leaving a ½-inch layer in the bottom of the casserole. Nestle the wrapped hens in the hot salt in the casserole. Pour the remaining hot salt over, completely covering the hens.

Cover tightly and bake for 50 minutes. (The casserole can be removed from the oven and set aside for up to 30 minutes without the hens cooling off.) Using two wooden spoons, carefully remove each hen to a platter. Unwrap the hens, transfer to dinner plates, and serve immediately.

✗ *Makes 2 servings*

Louisiana Rice

Wild pecan rice doesn't contain pecan nuts, nor is it wild rice. It is a Louisiana-grown product that has hints of the other two ingredients in its own distinctive flavor. Here the rice is combined with the Cornish hen giblets to create an upscale version of that Cajun favorite "dirty rice," a delicious side dish with a very unromantic name.

Giblets and livers of two Cornish hens, trimmed
1 tablespoon unsalted butter
1 shallot, minced
½ cup wild pecan rice (available in specialty food stores and most supermarkets)
1 cup homemade chicken stock or canned low-sodium broth
¼ teaspoon dried thyme
¼ teaspoon salt
Pinch of cayenne pepper
2 tablespoons chopped fresh parsley

In a food processor fitted with the metal blade, process the giblets and livers until finely chopped.

In a small saucepan, melt the butter over medium heat. Add the chopped meat mixture with the shallot and cook, stirring often, until the mixture loses its raw look, about 3 minutes. Add the rice and stir for 1 minute. Add the chicken stock, thyme, salt, and cayenne and bring to a boil. Cover, reduce the heat to low, and simmer until all the liquid is absorbed, 12 to 15 minutes. Let the rice stand for 5 minutes. Transfer to a warmed serving dish, sprinkle with the parsley, and serve immediately.

✗ *Makes 2 generous servings*

Minted Baby Carrots and Sugar Snap Peas

A colorful accompaniment to your Cornish hens that features extra-special vegetables (for an extra-special meal) that may require a visit to your best greengrocer. However, the mint butter would be equally delicious tossed with regular cooked carrots and green beans.

5 ounces baby carrots, trimmed, but not peeled
4 ounces sugar snap peas, trimmed
2 teaspoons unsalted butter
2 teaspoons chopped fresh mint, or ½ teaspoon dried
⅛ teaspoon salt
⅛ teaspoon freshly ground white pepper

In a medium saucepan of lightly salted boiling water, cook the baby carrots until tender, 5 to 7 minutes. Using a slotted spoon, transfer the carrots to a bowl of iced water and cool slightly. While still warm, use your fingers to slip the peels off the carrots.

In the same boiling water, cook the sugar snap peas just until they turn a brighter shade of green, about 1 minute. (Do not overcook.) Drain immediately, rinse under cold water and drain again. (The vegetables can be prepared up to 8 hours ahead, covered, and refrigerated.) In a medium skillet, melt the butter over medium heat. Add the vegetables, mint, salt, and pepper and cook, stirring occasionally, just until heated through, 3 to 5 minutes. Transfer to a warmed serving dish and serve immediately.

✗ *Makes 2 generous servings*

Boston Lettuce and Radicchio Salad with Roquefort and Pears

During a leisurely, romantic dinner, I like to serve a crisp, palate-refreshing salad after the main course, allowing the opportunity to dawdle before dessert. This is the perfect salad to serve under the circumstances, as it includes fruit, cheese, and walnuts—a trio I love almost as much as dessert itself.

1½ tablespoons champagne vinegar or white-wine vinegar
⅛ teaspoon salt
Pinch of freshly ground black pepper
3 tablespoons imported walnut oil
3 tablespoons vegetable oil
1 small head Boston lettuce, cleaned and torn into bite-sized pieces
½ head radicchio, cleaned and torn into bite-sized pieces
1 ripe medium red Bartlett pear, unpeeled, quartered, cored, and thinly sliced
2 ounces Roquefort or blue cheese, crumbled
¼ cup toasted walnuts, coarsely chopped

In a small bowl, whisk the vinegar with the salt and pepper. Gradually whisk in the oils until smooth. (The dressing can be made up to 2 days ahead, covered and refrigerated.)

In a medium bowl, toss the lettuce and radicchio with the dressing. Divide between two chilled salad plates. Top with the pear slices, then sprinkle with the cheese and walnuts. Serve immediately.

✗ *Makes 2 salads*

Clementines and Raspberries in Grand Marnier

A holiday romantic dinner is the time to splurge on out-of-season delicacies like raspberries. This simply prepared dessert allows you to conserve your energies for the more physically demanding aspects of an intimate meal.

4 clementines, peel and pith removed, separated
    into segments
2 tablespoons orange-flavored liqueur, such as
    Grand Marnier
1 pint fresh raspberries
½ cup chilled champagne, approximately

In a small bowl, combine the clementines and Grand Marnier. Cover tightly and refrigerate until chilled, at least 2 hours and up to 8 hours. Spoon the oranges and liqueur into two chilled dessert bowls. Divide the raspberries between the bowls. Pour about ¼ cup of chilled champagne (from the bottle you are serving with dinner) into each bowl and serve immediately.

✕ *Serves 2*

Carrot and Apple Cake with Cream Cheese Frosting

Mocha Gâteau Londres

Apple Brown Betty with Rum Whipped Cream

Candy-Cane and Chocolate-Chunk Ice Cream

Golden Caramel Pears

Christmas Day Parfaits

Hot Coffee   Cognac   Asti Spumante

Chapter Fifteen

A Sugarplum Dessert Party for Twenty

Everyone's sweet tooth seems to become apparent during the holidays. A showstopping buffet of fabulous desserts can be an excellent way of entertaining. As all of these desserts can be prepared ahead, it is a easy way to feed a crowd, too. As far as beverages go, freshly made coffee and a few bottles of sparkling wine (especially an Italian Asti Spumante) are all the menu requires.

There are many opportunities to present your dessert buffet. My favorite time is after a weekend holiday performance of *Messiah* or the *Nutcracker Suite.* It can be a nice way to offer sustenance during a tree trimming, or serve it after caroling with friends.

Following pages, left to right: Carrot and Apple Cake with Cream Cheese Frosting, Mocha Gâteau Londres, Apple Brown Betty with Rum Whipped Cream

Carrot and Apple Cake with Cream Cheese Frosting

This is a surprisingly good cake, even without the customary quantities of butter and eggs.

1¾ cups sifted all-purpose flour

⅔ cup sifted whole-wheat flour

1 teaspoon baking powder

½ teaspoon baking soda

⅛ teaspoon salt

2 teaspoons ground cinnamon

½ teaspoon ground nutmeg

¾ cup packed light-brown sugar

3 tablespoons vegetable oil

2 large eggs

6 carrots, grated (2 cups)

1 Granny Smith apple, unpeeled, cored, and grated (1 cup)

2 tablespoons low-fat vanilla yogurt

1 teaspoon vanilla extract

CREAM CHEESE FROSTING

3 ounces cream cheese, softened

2 tablespoons unsalted butter, softened

½ cup plus 2 tablespoons confectioners' sugar

¼ teaspoon vanilla extract

12 pecan halves, for garnish

Preheat the oven to 350° F. Butter and flour a 10-inch-round springform cake pan.

Sift together the flours, baking powder, baking soda, salt, cinnamon, and nutmeg into a large bowl.

In a second bowl, whisk the sugar, oil, and eggs until well combined. Stir in the carrot, apple, yogurt, and vanilla. Stir the carrot mixture into the flour mixture until well combined. Pour the batter into the prepared pan and smooth the top. Bake for 30 to 40 minutes, until a cake tester inserted in the center comes out clean.

Remove the cake from the oven, place on a wire cake rack, and allow to cool completely in the pan.

To make the frosting: In a small bowl, using a hand-held electric mixer set at high speed, beat the cream cheese and butter until smooth. Beat in the confectioners' sugar and vanilla. Refrigerate the frosting until thick enough to pipe, if necessary.

Spread or pipe the frosting on the top. Place the pecan halves around the edge of the cake.

✗ *Serves 12*

Mocha Gâteau Londres

I am particularly fond of this cake, reminiscent of the finest desserts purveyed at the cafés of Budapest. I learned how to make it at the London Cordon Bleu School of Cookery many years ago, and I am pleased to see that whenever I serve it, my guests enjoy it as much as I do.

CAKE

¾ cup slivered almonds
4 large eggs
¾ cup sugar
1 teaspoon almond extract
1 teaspoon instant espresso powder (not granular instant coffee)
1 cup sifted all-purpose flour

FILLING

¾ cup heavy cream
2 tablespoons sugar
1 teaspoon instant espresso powder
1 teaspoon vanilla extract

½ cup apricot preserves
3 ounces bittersweet chocolate, either grated or made into chocolate curls

Preheat the oven to 375° F. Butter a 9-inch-round cake pan, and line the bottom with a waxed paper round. Dust the inside of the pan with flour; tap out the excess.

Spread the almonds in a single layer on a baking sheet and bake, stirring occasionally, until golden brown, 8 to 10 minutes. Cool completely. In a food processor or blender, pulse the almonds until finely ground, but not oily. Measure out ⅔ cup and discard the rest.

Place the eggs and sugar in a heatproof medium bowl. Set the bowl in a medium saucepan of very hot, not simmering, water. (The bottom of the bowl should touch the water.) Whisking constantly, heat until the sugar has dissolved and the eggs are very warm to the touch (100° to 110° F.), about 3 minutes. (Rub a dab of the mixture between your thumb and forefinger to feel for undissolved sugar.) Remove from the water.

Using a hand-held electric mixer set at high speed, beat the egg mixture until thick and tripled in volume, about 5 minutes. Beat in the almond extract and espresso powder. Using a balloon whisk or large rubber spatula, fold in the flour.

Transfer the batter to the prepared pan and spread evenly. Bake until a toothpick inserted in the center of the cake comes out clean, 20 to 25 minutes. Cool the cake in the pan on a wire cake rack for 5 minutes, then invert onto the rack. Carefully remove the waxed paper, reinvert, and cool completely. (The cake can be prepared up to 1 day ahead, covered with plastic wrap, and stored at room temperature.)

To make the filling: Beat the cream and sugar in a chilled medium bowl until just thickened. Add the instant coffee and vanilla and beat until thick.

Using a serrated knife, cut the cake horizontally into two even layers. Sandwich the whipped cream filling between the two layers.

In a small saucepan, bring the apricot preserves to a boil over low heat. Cook until slightly reduced, about 2 minutes. Strain the hot preserves through a wire sieve into a bowl, discarding the solids in the sieve. Spread the top of the cake with the warm preserves. Let cool completely, then garnish the top of the cake with the chocolate. (The completed cake can be prepared up to 1 day ahead, loosely covered with plastic wrap, and refrigerated. Stand a few toothpicks into the top of the cake so the wrap will not touch the glaze and stick.) Serve the cake chilled.

✖ *Makes 8 servings*

Apple Brown Betty with Rum Whipped Cream

Every one loves brown betty, so make 2 or more of them to be sure there will be enough for everyone. This is equally mouth-watering prepared with pears.

APPLE BROWN BETTY

1 cup all-purpose flour

¼ teaspoon salt

½ teaspoon ground cinnamon

¼ teaspoon ground nutmeg

¾ cup sugar

8 tablespoons (1 stick) unsalted butter, chilled, cut into ½-inch pieces

4 slices firm-textured bread, crusts removed

1 cup raisins

3 Granny Smith apples, peeled, cored, and cut into ½-inch pieces (about 1½ pounds)

RUM WHIPPED CREAM

1 cup heavy cream

2 tablespoons sugar

2 tablespoons dark rum

To make the apple brown betty: Preheat the oven to 350°F. Butter a 9-inch-square baking dish.

Sift the flour, salt, cinnamon, nutmeg, and sugar into a bowl. Cut the butter into small pieces; cut it into the flour mixture, using a pastry blender, until the mixture resembles coarse crumbs.

Cut the bread into 1-inch-square pieces. Soak the raisins in boiling water to cover for about 5 minutes, until plump, then drain them. Combine the bread, raisins, and sliced apples in a bowl. Sprinkle the bottom of the prepared baking dish with ¾ cup of the flour mixture, add the apple mixture, and top with the remaining flour mixture.

Bake, uncovered, in the preheated oven until the top of the brown betty is crisp and golden and the apples are tender, 35 to 45 minutes.

To make the rum whipped cream: In a chilled medium bowl, beat the cream and sugar until stiff. Beat in the rum.

Serve the betty warm, with the rum whipped cream.

✗ *Serves 6*

Candy-Cane and Chocolate-Chunk Ice Cream

What is Christmas without peppermint candy canes? As for chocolate—although we enjoy it all year, what better excuse than the holidays to indulge?

10 ounces candy canes or hard peppermint
     candies, unwrapped
4 cups half-and-half
6 large egg yolks
3 ounces bittersweet chocolate, coarsely chopped

In a food processor fitted with the metal blade or a blender, process 6 ounces of the candy canes until finely crushed. You should have about 1 cup. Place the remaining 4 ounces of candy canes in a paper bag. Using a rolling pin or a meat pounder, coarsely crush the candy canes. You should have about ⅔ cup of coarsely crushed candy canes.

In a medium saucepan, combine the 1 cup finely crushed candy canes with the half-and-half. Stirring constantly to dissolve the candy, bring to a simmer over low heat.

In a medium bowl, whisk the egg yolks to combine. Gradually whisk the hot mixture into the egg yolks. Return the yolk mixture to the saucepan. Cook over low heat, stirring constantly with a wooden spoon, until the custard lightly coats the spoon, 4 to 5 minutes. (A thermometer inserted in the custard will read 180° to 185° F.) Strain the custard immediately into a medium bowl. Cool to room temperature, then cover, and refrigerate until very cold, at least 4 hours or overnight.

Transfer the custard to the container of an ice-cream maker, and freeze according to the manufacturer's instructions. Stir in the ⅔ cup coarsely crushed candy canes and the chopped chocolate.

Transfer to a 2-quart metal ice-cream mold or bowl. Place a piece of plastic wrap directly on the surface of the ice cream. Freeze until solid, at least 6 hours or overnight.

✖ *Makes about 1 ½ quarts*

Golden Caramel Pears

These small golden pears make a dazzling centerpiece at the dessert table. Sliced with a sharp paring knife and shared around the table, they are a wonderful accompaniment to coffee and conversation.

12 firm Seckel pears with stems
½ cup finely ground toasted hazelnuts
⅔ cup sugar
⅔ cup dark corn syrup
⅔ cup heavy cream
2 tablespoons unsalted butter
1 teaspoon vanilla extract
3 ounces semisweet chocolate, finely chopped

Line the pears up on a tray lined with parchment paper or aluminum foil. Place the ground nuts in a cup.

In a 1-quart pot, combine the sugar, corn syrup, cream, and butter. Using a wet pastry brush, wash down the sides of the pot to dissolve any sugar crystals. Over medium-high heat, bring the mixture to a boil and insert a candy thermometer. Stirring occasionally and washing down the sides of the pot, cook the mixture until it reaches 240° F. Immediately remove the pot from the heat and stir in the vanilla.

Holding a pear by the stem, tip the pot and dip the pear into the hot caramel, rotating the fruit to coat evenly all around. As you lift the pear out of the caramel, scrape the bottom along the edge of the pot, letting the excess drip back into the pot. Dip the pear into the nuts and set on the prepared tray. Repeat with the remaining pears, working as quickly as possible. Use a rubber spatula to scrape down the sides of the pot for the last few pears.

Fill the same small pot with about 1 inch of water and place over medium-high heat to simmer. Put about ⅔ of the chocolate in a small bowl and set over the pot, being careful not to let the water touch the bowl. When the chocolate is three quarters melted, remove the bowl from the pot, add the remaining chocolate, and stir to melt completely. Using a teaspoon, spoon the chocolate over the top of each pear, nudging it a little with the back of the spoon to drip down the sides of the fruit. Set the tray in a cool dry place until the chocolate hardens completely, and then leave at room temperature. Serve the pears the same day.

✖ *Makes 12 servings*

Christmas Day Parfaits

This ice-cream sundae has a Yuletide color scheme to match its holiday flavors. Vanilla ice cream is layered with warm chocolate mint sauce and lightly cooked raspberries, and then garnished with fresh mint. If mint is not your cup of tea, it may be omitted from the chocolate sauce.

3 cups raspberries
1 bunch fresh mint
3 to 4 tablespoons sugar (or to taste)
2 tablespoons water
1¼ cups heavy cream
5 peppermint tea bags
10 ounces high-quality semisweet chocolate,
      coarsely chopped
1½ pints vanilla ice cream

Set aside about 18 raspberries and 6 sprigs of fresh mint for garnish.

Combine the sugar and water in a pot and add the remaining raspberries. Stir gently to coat the berries with the liquid. Cover the pot and, over medium heat, cook the berries just until they soften but do not lose their shape, stirring occasionally, 3 to 4 minutes. Remove from heat.

Take the remaining fresh mint leaves off their stems and chop coarsely. In a medium pot, over medium-high heat, scald the cream. Remove from heat and add the tea bags along with the fresh mint leaves. Let steep until the cream is completely cool. Squeeze the tea bags out into the cream, strain it, and return the cream to the pot. Put the pot back on the heat and scald it again. Remove from heat and stir in the chopped chocolate until it is completely melted. This sauce can be made in advance and then heated up at the last minute.

Line up 6 parfait or pilsner glasses and put a tablespoon of the raspberry sauce in the bottom of each. Layer the ice cream, chocolate mint sauce, and raspberry sauce twice, ending with the raspberry sauce on top. Add a few uncooked raspberries and garnish with the fresh mint sprigs.

✕ *Serves 6*

INDEX

INDEX

225